JN438186

미국법 시리즈

Real Property

미국 부동산법

강병진 저

법률신문사

| PREFACE |

이 책은 미국 부동산법(Real Property)에 대한 전반적인 해설서로서 미국 부동산법을 이해하기 쉬운 방식으로 설명하는 데 목적을 두고 있습니다. 그 동안 미국 부동산법을 강의하면서 정리해 두었던 강의안을 정리하여 출판하게 되었습니다.

이 책에서 다루는 미국 부동산법은 크게 토지에 대한 권리(Estates in Land), 임대인과 임차인(Landlord and Tenant), 점유취득시효(Adverse Possession), 토지 양도(Land Conveyance), 저당권(Mortgages), 타인의 토지에 대한 권리(Rights to the Land of Another), 토지 소유권에 부수하는 권리(Rights Incidental to Land Ownership), 기타 사항(Other Matters)에 대한 내용으로 이루어져 있습니다. 위의 사항들에 대한 주요 내용을 상세히 다루고, 부동산법에 대한 전반적인 내용을 학습할 수 있도록 구성하였습니다.

이 책은 미국 부동산법의 기본 내용을 체계적으로 학습하고자 하는 분들을 위한 책입니다. 특히, 미국변호사 자격을 취득하고자 하는 분들은 이 책을 통해 시험에 필요한 이론들을 체계적으로 학습할 수 있는 교재로 활용할 수 있을 겁니다. 미국 로스쿨 입학을 앞두고 있는 분들은 기본적인 지식을 얻는 준비서로서 부동산법에 대한 용어에 익숙해질 수 있는 기회가 될 것이고, 미국법을 학습하고자 하는 분들은 미국 부동산법에 대한 전반적인 이론을 접하는 학습서로서 활용할 수 있을 겁니다.

이 책 내용의 서술은 영어 원문과 한국어 설명을 덧붙이는 방식으로 하였습니다. 영어 원문을 통해서 관련 법리를 이해하고 익히기를 바랍니다. 한국어 설명은 영어 원문의 이해를 돕는 데 활용할 수 있을 겁니다. 이 책을 통해 미국의 부동산법을 학습하는 방법은 본문에 나오는 각 법리들에 대한 영어 원문의 의미를 우선 이해하고 내용에 익숙해지게 끔 학습하는 것이 중요합니다. 영어 원문은 박스안에 기재를 해서 식별이 잘 되게끔 하였습니다. 영어 원문의 법 이론에 대한 이해는 한국어 설명을 보면 이해에 도움이 될 것입니다. 영어 원문과 한국어 설명에는 미국 연방대법원의 판례 및 미국변호사 시험에 자주 등장하는 사례와 예시들이 있으니 잘 읽어 보기를 권합니다.

법률 용어에 대한 한국어 번역이나 설명을 할 때 최대한 미국법 용어와 유사한 용어를 선택하려고 노력했습니다. 그러나 한국어 용어가 적절하지 않거나 부자연스러운 부분이 있을 수도 있을 것이라 생각이 됩니다. 이런 부분은 확인이 되면 고치고 보완하도록 하겠습니다.

미국법을 공부하거나 미국변호사 시험을 준비하는 이들에게 이 책이 좋은 길잡이가 되길 바라며, 이미 미국법에 대한 이해가 있는 분들에게는 좀더 깊은 지식을 제공하고 이해의 폭을 넓히는 데 도움이 되기를 희망해 봅니다. 나아가 여러분의 미국법 학습 여정에 있어 이 책과 앞으로 집필해서 출간하게 되는 미국법 책들이 신뢰할 수 있는 좋은 동반자가 되기를 바랍니다.

이 책을 출간하는 데 도움을 주신 법률신문 출판팀과 교육팀 여러분에게 깊은 감사를 드립니다.

| CONTENTS |

REAL PROPERTY

미국 부동산법

—

REAL PROPERTY

I | 토지에 대한 권리(ESTATES IN LAND)

Estates in land are possessory interests in land. These interests may be presently possessory (present estates)[1] or they may be possessory in the future (future interests)[2]. They may be freeholds, which give possession under some legal title or right to hold (e.g., life estate), or they may be non-freeholds, which give mere possession (i.e., lease).

Estates in land may be of potentially infinite duration, as in the case of a fee simple, or they may be of limited duration, as in the case of an estate for years. But whatever their characteristics, estates in land must be distinguished from non-possessory interests such as easements, profits, covenants, and servitudes.

토지에 대한 권리(estates in land)는 토지에 대한 점유권을 의미하며, 현재 점유할 수 있는 권리(현재의 권리)일 수도 있고, 미래에 점유할 수 있는 권리(미래의 권리)일 수도 있다. 이러한 권리는 법적 권리에 따라 점유할 수 있는 자유보유권(종신소유권)일 수 있으며, 단순한 점유를 갖는 비자유보유권(임대차)일 수도 있다.

토지에 대한 권리는 단순 소유권인 경우 영구적일 수 있고, 확정기한부 소유권처럼 일정 기간으로 한정될 수도 있다. 그러나 이러한 특성에 관계없이, 토지에 대한 권리는 지역권, 수익권, 약정 또는 부담권과 같은 비점유 권리와는 구별된다.

---

1) Estate는 부동산에 대한 현재의 소유권, 점유권, 사용권 등을 포괄하는 법적 개념이다. 이는 해당 부동산에 대한 현재의 실질적이고 직접적인 권리를 의미한다. Present Estate는 이름에서 알 수 있듯이 현재 시점에서 점유를 할 수 있는 권리를 나타낸다. 예를 들어, "fee simple estate"나 "life estate"와 같은 현재 점유를 할 수 있는 권리 형태를 지칭한다.

2) Interest는 부동산에 대한 다양한 형태의 권리를 포괄하는 보다 광범위한 용어이다. 이는 현재뿐만 아니라 미래에 발생할 수 있는 권리도 포함한다. Future Interest는 현재는 점유를 하고 있지 않지만, 미래의 어느 시점에 점유를 할 수 있는 권리를 의미한다. 예를 들어, "remainder interest"나 "executory interest"와 같이 미래의 어느 시점에 점유를 할 수 있는 권리를 지칭한다.

A 현재의 권리(Present Estates)

1. 절대적 단순 소유권(Fee Simple Absolute)

Fee simple absolute is the most complete and extensive form of property ownership recognized in real property law. It represents the broadest interest one can have in land, offering the owner absolute and unrestricted rights over the property.

1) Absolute Ownership of Potentially Infinite Duration

A fee simple absolute estate is of potentially infinite duration. This means the ownership can last forever and is not subject to any conditions that might limit its duration. The estate continues as long as there are heirs to inherit the property, and it does not terminate on any specific event other than the absence of heirs.

2) Freely Alienable

The fee simple absolute estate is fully transferable. The owner can freely sell, gift, or bequeath the property without any restrictions. This characteristic makes it the most flexible and marketable form of property ownership, facilitating the easy transfer of property in real estate transactions.

3) No Accompanying Future Interest

In a fee simple absolute, there are no future interests attached to the property. This means that there are no remainders, reversions, or other contingent interests that would follow the present estate. The owner has full and complete ownership without any other parties holding a legal interest in the property that could arise in the future.

4) Modern Interpretations

Historically, common law required specific words of limitation ("and heirs") in the conveyance to create a fee simple absolute. However, modern property law has evolved, and courts now presume a fee simple absolute when a conveyance is ambiguous or does not specify a lesser estate. For instance, a deed that simply conveys property "to B" is interpreted as granting a fee simple absolute by default.

5) Examples of Fee Simple Absolute

Example: A conveys Blackacre "to B and his heirs." This language explicitly grants B a fee simple absolute estate in Blackacre, with the term "and his heirs" indicating that the estate is of potentially infinite duration and can be inherited by B's descendants.

Example: C conveys Greenacre "to B." Even without the traditional "and his heirs" language, this conveyance is interpreted as granting B a fee simple absolute estate in Greenacre because modern law presumes this form of ownership in the absence of explicit limitations.

절대적 단순 소유권은 부동산법에서 인정되는 가장 완전하고 포괄적인 형태의 재산권이다. 이는 토지에 대한 가장 넓은 범위의 권리를 의미하며, 소유권자에게 재산에 대한 절대적이고 제한 없는 권리를 제공한다.

1) 잠재적으로 무한한 기간의 절대적 소유권
(Absolute Ownership of Potentially Infinite Duration)

절대적 단순 소유권은 잠재적으로 무한한 기간 동안 지속될 수 있는 소유권이다. 이는 소유권이 영원히 지속될 수 있으며, 기간을 제한할 수 있는 어떠한 조건에도 종속되지 않는다는 것을 의미한다. 이 소유권은 상속인이 존재하는 한 계속되며, 상속인의 부재 외에는 특정한 사건에 의해 종료되지 않는다.

2) 자유로운 양도(Freely Alienable)

절대적 단순 소유권은 완전하게 양도가 가능하다. 소유권자는 재산을 자유롭게 매각, 증여 또는 유증할 수 있으며, 이에 대한 어떠한 제한도 없다. 이 특성은 절대적 단순 소유권을 가장 유연하고 거래 가능한 재산 소유 형태로 만들어 부동산 거래에서 재산의 용이한 이전을 가능하게 한다.

3) 미래의 권리 부존재(No Accompanying Future Interest)

절대적 단순 소유권에는 재산에 부속된 미래의 권리가 없다. 이는 현재 소유권 뒤에 따라오는 잔여권, 복귀권 또는 기타 조건부 권리가 없다는 것을 의미한다. 소유권자는 재산에 대해 완전하고 완벽한 소유권을 가지며, 미래에 발생할 수 있는 법적 권리를 가진 다른 당사자가 존재하지 않는다.

4) 현대적 해석(Modern Interpretations)

역사적으로 보통법은 절대적 단순 소유권을 설정하기 위해서는 양도 문서에 일정한 제한적 언어("and heirs")가 필요했다. 그러나 현대 부동산법에서는 양도가 모호하거나 더 작은 소유권이 명시되지 않은 경우에는 법원이 절대적 단순 소유권으로 추정하는 것이 일반적이다. 예를 들어, "to B"라는 간단한 표현으로 재산을 양도하는 문서는 기본적으로 절대적 단순 소유권을 부여하는 것으로 해석된다.

5) 절대적 단순 소유권의 예시(Examples of Fee Simple Absolute)

예시: A conveys Blackacre "to B and his heirs." 이 문구는 명시적으로 B에게 토지에 대한 절대적 단순 소유권을 부여하며, "and his heirs" 용어는 이 소유권이 잠재적으로 무한한 기간 동안 지속되며 B의 후손에게 상속될 수 있음을 나타낸다.

예시: A conveys Greenacre "to B." 전통적인 "and his heirs"라는 표현이 없더라도, 이 양도는 B에게 토지에 대한 절대적 단순 소유권을 부여하는 것으로 해석된다.

2. 조건부 소유권(Defeasible Fees)

Defeasible fees are types of fee simple estates that, like a fee simple absolute, involve ownership of potentially infinite duration. However, unlike a fee simple absolute, a defeasible fee may be terminated upon the occurrence of a specific event or condition. These estates are categorized into three main types: fee simple determinable, fee simple subject to condition subsequent, and fee simple subject to executory interest.

조건부 소유권(defeasible fees)은 절대적 단순 소유권처럼 잠재적으로 무한한 기간 동안 소유할 수 있는 단순 소유권이다. 그러나 절대적 단순 소유권과는 달리, 조건부 소유권은 특정 사건이나 조건이 발생하면 종료될 수 있다. 이러한 소유권은 크게 세 가지 유형으로 나뉜다. 즉 기간조건부 단순 소유권(fee simple determinable), 해제조건부 단순 소유권(fee simple subject to condition subsequent) 및 제3자 이전 조건부 단순 소유권(fee simple subject to executory interest)이다.

1) 기간조건부 단순 소유권(Fee simple determinable)

A fee simple determinable is a present fee simple estate that is subject to specific conditions, as indicated by durational language. It is characterized by automatic termination upon the occurrence of a specified event, at which point ownership reverts to the grantor without any further action required.

a) Durational Language: A fee simple determinable is created by using specific durational language (e.g., so long as, while, during, until) in the conveyance.

b) Automatic Termination: The estate automatically ends upon the occurrence of the stated condition, and ownership of the property reverts back to the grantor without any need for legal action or re-entry.

c) Freely Alienable, Devisable, and Descendible: a fee simple determinable is freely alienable, devisable, and descendible. However, it is always subject to the stated condition, meaning that the estate can still terminate if the specified event occurs, even after being transferred.

d) Possibility of Reverter: The grantor's future interest in a fee simple determinable is called a possibility of reverter. This is the interest that the grantor retains in case the condition that terminates the estate occurs. The possibility of reverter can be transferred by the grantor during his lifet or upon his death.

e) Example: O conveys Blackacre "to A so long as it is used as a park." In this example, A holds a fee simple determinable in Blackacre. If A converts the land to a shopping center, A's estate terminates automatically, and the property reverts to O. O retains a possibility of reverter, meaning that ownership of Blackacre will return to O upon A's marriage.

기간조건부 단순 소유권(fee simple determinable)은 특정 조건에 종속되는 현재 단순 소유권으로, 기간의 표현에 의해 그 조건이 명시된다. 특정 사건이 발생하면 소유권이 자동으로 종료되며, 이때 소유권은 양도인에게 자동으로 반환된다.

a) 기간의 언어(Durational Language): 기간조건부 단순 소유권은 기간의 언어(예: so long as, while, during, until)를 사용하여 설정한다.

b) 자동 종료(Automatic Termination): 명시된 조건이 발생하면 소유권은 자동으로 종료되며, 법적 조치나 재진입 없이 소유권이 양도인에게 자동으로 반환된다.

c) 자유로운 양도 가능(Freely Alienable, Devisable, and Descendible):

기간조건부 단순 소유권은 자유롭게 양도, 유증, 상속될 수 있다. 그러나 명시된 조건에 항상 종속되므로, 소유권이 양도된 이후에도 특정 사건이 발생하면 소유권은 여전히 종료될 수 있다.

Alienable의 의미는 생전 양도(transfer by inter vivos), devisable의 의미는 유언서에 의한 양도(transfer by a will), descendible의 의미는 유언서 없이 상속법에 따른 양도(transfer by intestacy)의 의미이다.[3]

d) 복귀가능권(Possibility of Reverter): 기간조건부 단순 소유권에서 양도인이 가지는 미래의 권리를 복귀가능권이라고 한다. 이는 조건이 충족되어 소유권이 종료될 경우 양도인이 소유권을 회복할 수 있는 권리이다. 복귀가능권은 양도인이 자유롭게 양도가 가능하여, 양도인이 생전에 양도하거나 사망시 양도될 수 있다.

e) 예시: O conveys Blackacre "to A so long as it is used as a park." A는 토지에 대한 기간조건부 단순 소유권을 가진다. 만약 A가 그 토지를 쇼핑 센터로 바꾸면, A의 소유권은 자동으로 종료되며 재산은 양도인에게 반환된다. 양도인은 복귀가능권을 보유하고 있으며, A가 결혼할 경우 토지의 소유권은 양도인에게 돌아온다.

2) 해제조건부 단순 소유권(Fee simple subject to a condition subsequent)

A fee simple subject to a condition subsequent is a present fee simple where ownership may be terminated if a specified condition is violated. Unlike a fee simple determinable, which terminates automatically upon the occurrence of a condition, a fee simple subject to a condition subsequent only terminates if the grantor affirmatively demonstrates the intent to terminate after the condition is met.

3) 유언서에 의한 양도나 상속법에 따른 양도에 대한 자세한 내용은 Trusts and Wills (미국 신탁 및 유언법, 2024.6, 강병진 저) 도서에 설명되어 있음.

a) Conditional Language: A fee simple subject to a condition subsequent is created by using specific conditional language (e.g., provided that, on condition that, but if) in the conveyance

b) Termination is Not Automatic: The key difference from a fee simple determinable is that the estate does not automatically terminate when the condition is met. The grantor must take affirmative action to terminate the estate, such as filing a legal claim to reenter the property.

c) Freely Alienable, Devisable, and Descendible: Like a fee simple determinable, a fee simple subject to a condition subsequent freely alienable by the owner during his life, and upon his death, it is devisable and descendible. However, it remains subject to the condition, meaning that the estate can still be terminated if the condition occurs and the grantor exercises their right of termination.

d) Right of Entry or Power of Termination: The grantor retains a future interest called a right of entry (also known as a "power of termination"), which allows the grantor to reclaim the property if the condition is breached. To reclaim the property, the grantor must explicitly act to exercise the right of entry. The grantor may waive their right of entry, but mere inaction (failure to assert the right) does not automatically constitute a waiver.

e) Example: O conveys Blackacre "to A on the condition that it be used for educational purposes." In this example, A holds a fee simple subject to a condition subsequent in Blackacre. The condition is that A should use the Blackacre for educational purposes. If the school later decides to use the property for commercial purposes, the grantor (or the grantor's heirs) would have the right to reclaim the property, but only if they choose to exercise that right by filing an action for re-entry. The property would not automatically revert to the grantor.

해제조건부 단순 소유권(fee simple subject to a condition subsequent)은 특정 조건이 위반될 경우 소유권이 종료될 수 있는 현재 단순 소유권이다. 기간조건부 단순 소유권과 달리, 조건이 충족되면 자동으로 종료되지 않고, 양도인이 소유권을 종료하려는 의사를 적극적으로 명확히 해야만 소유권이 종료된다.

a) 조건적 언어(Conditional Language): 해제조건부 단순 소유권은 조건적 언어(예: provided that, on condition that, but if)를 사용하여 설정한다.

b) 자동 종료 안됨(Termination is Not Automatic): 기간조건부 단순 소유권과의 주요 차이점은 조건이 충족되더라도 소유권이 자동으로 종료되지 않는다는 점이다. 양도인이 소유권을 종료하려면 법적 청구 등을 통해 해당 재산을 다시 소유할 의사를 명확히 해야 한다.

c) 자유로운 양도(Freely Alienable, Devisable, and Descendible): 해제조건부 단순 소유권은 기간조건부 단순 소유권처럼 자유롭게 생전 양도나 사후 양도를 할 수 있다. 그러나 조건에 종속되므로, 조건이 충족되면 양도인의 종료권 행사로 여전히 소유권이 종료될 수 있다.

d) 진입권(Right of Entry or Power of Termination): 양도인은 진입권을 보유하며, 조건이 위반될 경우 재산을 회수할 수 있는 권리를 가진다. 재산을 회수하려면 양도인이 명확히 진입권을 행사해야 한다. 그러나 단순히 미래의 권리의 권리를 주장하지 않는다고 해서 자동으로 이 권리를 포기하는 것으로 간주되지는 않는다.

e) 예시: O conveys Blackacre "to A on the condition that it be used for educational purposes." A는 토지에 대한 해제조건부 단순 소유권을 가진다. 조건은 A가 토지를 교육 목적으로 사용해야 한다는 것이다. 나중에 학교가 해당 재산을 상업적 목적으로 사용하기로 결정하면, 양도인은 진입권을 행사하여 재산을 회수할 수 있는 권리가 생긴다. 하지만 이때 재산이 자동으로 양도인에게 반환되는 것은 아니며, 양도인이 재진입을 위한 조치 등을 취해야만 한다.

3) 제3자 이전 조건부 단순 소유권 (Fee simple subject to an executory interest)

A fee simple subject to an executory interest (also known as a fee simple subject to an executory limitation) is a present fee simple estate that is limited in duration by either durational language or conditional language. Upon the occurrence of a specified condition, ownership does not revert to the grantor but instead automatically transfers to a third party who holds an executory interest.

a) Durational or Conditional Language: This estate is created using either durational or conditional language.

b) Automatic Termination: Upon the occurrence of the specified event or condition, the estate automatically terminates, but instead of reverting to the grantor, the property passes directly to a designated third party.

c) Freely Alienable, Devisable, and Descendible: A fee simple subject to an executory interest freely alienable by the owner during his life, and upon his death, it is devisable and descendible.

d) Executory Interest: The third party's future interest is called an executory interest, which becomes possessory upon the occurrence of the condition. The key distinction between this estate and other defeasible estates is the involvement of a third party, who will take ownership of the property if a specified event occurs.

e) Example: O conveys Blackacre "to A, but if A sells alcohol on the property, then to B." In this case, A holds a fee simple subject to an executory interest. A's estate in Blackacre will last but if A sells alcohol, the property will automatically transfer to B.

제3자 이전 조건부 단순 소유권(fee simple subject to an executory interest)은 현재 단순 소유권으로, 기간의 언어 또는 조건적 언어에 의해 그 소유권의 보유 기간이 제한된다. 특정 조건이 발생하면 소유권은 양도인에게 복귀되지 않고, 대신 제3자에게 자동으로 이전된다.

a) 기간의 또는 조건적 언어(Durational or Conditional Language): 이 소유권은 기간의 또는 조건적 언어를 사용하여 설정한다.

b) 자동 종료(Automatic Termination): 명시된 사건이나 조건이 발생하면 소유권은 자동으로 종료되며, 재산은 양도인에게 반환되지 않고 지정된 제3자에게 자동으로 이전된다.

c) 자유로운 양도(Freely Alienable, Devisable, and Descendible): 제3자 이전 조건부 단순 소유권은 자유롭게 생전 양도나 사후 양도를 할 수 있다.

d) 미확정 미래의 권리(Executory Interest): 제3자의 미래의 권리는 미확정 미래의 권리이라 하며, 어떤 조건이 발생하면 제3자가 재산에 대한 소유권을 취득하게 된다. 이 소유권과 다른 조건부 소유권들의 주요 차이점은 특정 사건이 발생하면 제3자가 소유권을 취득한다는 점이다.

e) 예시: O conveys Blackacre "to A, but if A sells alcohol on the property, then to B." A는 제3자 이전 조건부 단순 소유권을 가진다. A의 토지에 대한 소유권은 유지되지만, A가 그 재산에서 술을 판매하면 재산은 자동으로 B에게 이전된다.

3. 상속 제한부 소유권(Fee Tail)

The fee tail is a type of freehold estate that historically limited inheritance of the property to the grantee's direct lineal descendants. This form of estate was designed to keep property within a family line, ensuring that the land would be passed down through generations of the same bloodline.

A fee tail estate restricts inheritance to the grantee's direct descendants, often specified by words of limitation such as "to A and the heirs of her body." This means that only the grantee's children, grandchildren, and further direct descendants could inherit the property.

The fee tail estate has been largely abolished in the United States and other common law jurisdictions. In most states, a conveyance that would have created a fee tail at common law is now interpreted as creating a fee simple absolute.

Example: O conveys Blackacre "to A and the heirs of her body." Under old common law, this language would create a fee tail. However, in most modern jurisdictions, this conveyance would instead be interpreted as granting A a fee simple absolute.

상속 제한부 소유권은 역사적으로 재산 상속을 양수인의 직계 후손으로 제한하는 형태의 자유보유권이다. 이 소유권 형태는 재산이 같은 혈통의 후손들에게 대대로 전해지도록 설계되어, 가족 내에서 재산이 유지되도록 하는 목적을 가지고 있다.

상속 제한부 소유권은 상속을 양수인의 직계 후손으로 제한하며, "to A and the heirs of her body."와 같은 제한적 표현에 의해 종종 명시된다. 이는 양수인의 자녀, 손자 및 더 먼 직계 후손들만이 재산을 상속받을 수 있음을 의미한다.

상속 제한부 소유권은 미국과 다른 보통법 관할권에서 대부분 폐지되었다. 대부분의 주에서는, 보통법상의 상속 제한부 소유권은 절대적 단순 소유권을 설정한 것으로 해석된다.

예시: A conveys Blackacre "to B and the heirs of her body." 과거의 보통법 하에서는 이 표현이 상속 제한부 소유권을 성립했을 것이다. 그러나 현재 이 양도는 B에게 절대적 단순 소유권을 부여하는 것으로 해석된다.

4. 종신소유권(Life Estate)

1) 일반원칙(General rule)

A life estate is a present possessory estate in real property that lasts for the duration of a person's life, referred to as the measuring life. It grants the life tenant the right to use, possess, and derive benefits from the property during their lifetime, but it terminates upon the death of the individual whose life is used as the measuring standard. Upon termination, the property either reverts to the grantor or passes to a third party (remainderman), depending on the terms of the conveyance.

a) Measuring Life

The life estate must be clearly defined by the life of an individual, not a specific number of years. The most common example is language such as "to A for life," which means A has the right to use the property during their lifetime. Upon the death of the person whose life is used as the measuring standard, the estate ends.

b) Termination and Reversion/Remainder

When the measuring life ends, the property automatically reverts to the grantor (known as a reversion) or passes to a third party (known as a remainder).

Example: A conveys Blackacre "to B for the life of B." Upon B's death, Blackacre reverts to A.

Example: A conveys Blackacre "to B for B's life, and then to C." Upon B's death, Blackacre passes to C, the remainderman.

c) Not Subject to the Rule Against Perpetuities

Life estates are not subject to the Rule Against Perpetuities because their duration is inherently tied to a human lifespan, which ensures they will end within a determinable period.

d) Types of Life Estates

i) Measuring Life is the Grantee

In most life estates, the measuring life is the life of the grantee (life tenant). For example, A conveys Blackacre "to B for life." B's life is the measuring life, and the estate terminates upon B's death.

Transferability: A life estate can be transferred during the lifetime of the life tenant, but the transferred interest still ends upon the death of the measuring life. As a result, a life estate is generally not devisable (transferable by will) or descendible (inheritable by the grantee's heirs).

ii) Measuring Life is a Third Party (Life Estate Pur Autre Vie)

A life estate measured by the life of someone other than the grantee is called a life estate pur autre vie. For example, A conveys Blackacre "to B for the life of C." B holds a life estate that is measured by C's life. When C dies, the estate terminates, regardless of whether B is still alive.

종신소유권(life estate)은 부동산에 대한 현재 점유 소유권으로, 특정 개인의 일생 동안 지속된다. 종신소유권자는 살아있는 동안 재산을 사용하고 점유하며 그로부터 이익을 얻을 권리를 가진다. 그러나 특정 개인 즉 기준생애가 되는 자의 사망 시 종신소유권은 종료되며, 재산은 양도인에게 복귀되거나 제3자(잔여권리자)에게 이전된다.

a) 기준생애(Measuring Life)

종신소유권은 특정 개인의 생애로 명확히 정의되어야 하며, 특정 연수로 제한되지 않는다. 가장 일반적인 예는 "to A for life"라는 표현이다. 이는 A가 생애 동안 재산을 사용할 권리가 있음을 의미하며, 기준생애가 되는 자의 사망 시 소유권은 종료된다.

b) 종료 및 복귀권/잔여권(Termination and Reversion/Remainder)

기준생애가 종료하는 경우, 재산은 자동으로 양도인에게 복귀되거나(복귀권) 제3자에게 이전(잔여권) 된다.

예시: A conveys Blackacre "to B for the life of B." B가 사망하면 토지는 A에게 복귀한다.

예시: A conveys Blackacre "to B for B's life, and then to C." B가 사망하면 토지는 잔여권자인 C에게 이전된다.

c) 영구불확정금지 원칙 적용 제외(Not Subject to the Rule Against Perpetuities)

종신소유권은 그 기간이 인간의 수명에 의해 결정되므로, 영구불확정금지 원칙의 적용을 받지 않는다.

d) 종신소유권의 유형(Types of Life Estates)

i) 기준생애가 양수인인 경우(Measuring Life is the Grantee)

대부분의 종신소유권에서 기준생애는 양수인의 생애이다. 예를 들어, A conveys Blackacre "to B for life."인 경우 양수인인 B의 생애가 기준생애가 되고, B가 사망하면 종신소유권은 종료된다.

양도성(Transferability): 종신소유권은 종신소유권자가 생존하는 동안 양도될 수 있으나, 양도된 권리는 기준생애가 종료되면 여전히 종료된다. 따라서 종신소유권은 일반적으로 상속되지 않는다.

ii) 기준생애가 제3자일 경우 (Measuring Life is a Third Party)

기준생애가 양수인이 아닌 제3자의 생애로 설정된 종신소유권은 타인의 생애에 의한 종신소유권(life estate pur autre vie)이라고 한다. 예를 들어, A conveys Blackacre "to B for the life of C."인 경우 C의 생애가 기준생애가 되고, C가 사망하면 B가 생존하고 있더라도 종신소유권은 종료된다.

2) 종신소유권자의 권리 및 의무(Rights and Obligations of the Life Tenant)

a) Rights of the Life Tenant

The life tenant has the right to possess and use the property for their lifetime. The life tenant is entitled to all rents and profits generated from the property during their possession. The life tenant can lease, sell, or mortgage their interest in the property but any transferred interest will still terminate upon the death of the measuring life.

b) Obligations of the Life Tenant

The life tenant must pay all ordinary property taxes and interest on any mortgage during their possession. If the property generates income, the life tenant is responsible for paying these obligations from that income. If the property does not generate income, the life tenant must pay taxes and interest up to the reasonable rental value of the property. The life tenant has a duty to avoid waste, which includes actions or inactions that reduce the value of the property.

a) 종신소유권자의 권리(Rights of the Life Tenant)

종신소유권자는 자신의 생애 동안 부동산을 점유하고 사용할 권리를 가진다. 종신소유권자는 점유 기간 동안 부동산에서 발생하는 모든 임대료와 수익을 받을 권리가 있으며, 자신의 권리를 임대, 매각 또는 담보로 설정할 수 있지만, 그러한 권리는 기준생애를 갖는 자가 사망하면 종료된다.

b) 종신소유권자의 의무(Obligations of the Life Tenant)

종신소유권자는 부동산 점유 기간 동안 모든 일반적인 재산세와 저당권 이자의 지급 의무를 가진다. 부동산에서 수익이 발생하는 경우, 종신소유권자는 그 수익으로 이러한 의무를 이행해야 한다. 만약 부동산이 수익을 발생시키지 않는다면, 종신소유권자는 해당 재산의 합리적인 임대

가치에 해당하는 범위 내에서 세금과 이자를 지불해야 한다. 종신소유권자는 부동산의 가치를 훼손시키는 행위(작위 또는 부작위)를 방지할 의무가 있다.

3) 훼손행위의 원칙(Doctrine of waste)

The life tenant's rights to use the property are limited by the doctrine of waste, which protects the interests of future owners (remaindermen or reversioners).

a) Affirmative (Voluntary) Waste

Affirmative waste occurs when the life tenant takes actions that cause permanent damage to the property or reduce its value (e.g., destroying buildings, overharvesting timber).

Exceptions may apply if the grantor authorized such activities, they were customary at the time of the tenancy, or they are necessary to maintain the property.

b) Permissive Waste

Permissive waste results from the life tenant's failure to maintain the property, leading to neglect and deterioration. This includes failing to repair the property, pay taxes, or protect it from damage.

The life tenant's responsibility for permissive waste is limited to the amount of income generated by the property.

c) Ameliorative Waste

Ameliorative waste occurs when the life tenant makes changes to the property that increase its value but alter its original character or structure.

Under modern law, ameliorative waste is allowed if the alterations are reasonable and necessary for the property's use, even if future interest holders (remaindermen or reversioners) do not consent.

종신소유권자의 부동산 사용 권리는 훼손행위의 원칙에 의해 제한되며, 이는 미래권리자(잔여권자 또는 복귀권자)의 권리를 보호하기 위한 것이다.

a) 적극적 훼손행위(Affirmative Waste)

적극적 훼손행위는 종신소유권자가 부동산에 영구적인 훼손을 하거나 가치를 감소시키는 행위를 하는 경우 발생한다(예: 건물 파괴, 과도한 벌목). 예외적으로 양도인이 이러한 행위를 허가했거나, 부동산을 양수받을 당시의 관습이었거나, 부동산 유지에 필요하다면 허용될 수 있다.

b) 소극적 훼손행위(Permissive Waste)

소극적 훼손행위는 종신소유권자가 부동산을 유지 관리하지 않아 방치되고 악화되는 경우 발생한다. 이는 수리 불이행, 세금 미납 또는 부동산 보호 소홀을 포함한다. 종신소유권자의 소극적 훼손행위에 대한 책임은 부동산에서 발생하는 수익의 범위 내로 제한된다.

c) 개량적 훼손행위(Ameliorative Waste)

개량적 훼손행위는 종신소유권자가 부동산의 가치를 증가시키지만 원래의 성격이나 구조를 변경하는 경우 발생한다. 현대법에서는 그러한 변경이 합리적이고 부동산 이용에 필요하다면, 잔여권자나 복귀권자의 동의가 없더라도 개량적 훼손행위는 허용되는 것으로 본다.

B 미래의 권리(Future Interest)

A future interest is an interest in presently existing property, which will or may commence in use, possession, or enjoyment sometime in the future. Future interests can be retained by the grantor or conveyed to third parties.

미래의 권리(future interest)는 현재 존재하는 재산에 대한 권리로, 미래에 사용, 점유 또는 향유가 시작될 수 있거나 시작될 가능성이 있는 권리를 의미한다. 미래의 권리는 양도인이 보유하거나 제3자에게 양도될 수 있다.

1. 복귀권(Reversion)

A reversion (or reverter) is the future interest retained by the grantor when they convey a life estate or estate for years but do not specify that the remaining future interest will go to a third party (a remainderman). In this case, the property automatically "reverts" back to the grantor upon the termination of the life estate or estate for years.

Example: If a grantor conveys property "to A for life," the grantor retains a reversion. When A dies, the property automatically reverts to the grantor or the grantor's heirs, as no third party has been designated to receive the property.

복귀권(reversion)은 양도인이 종신소유권(life estate) 또는 확정기한부 소유권(estate for years)을 양도할 때 양도인이 보유하는 미래의 권리다. 제3자가 미래의 권리를 보유하지는 않는다. 이 경우, 종신소유권 또는 확정기한부 소유권이 종료되면 재산은 자동으로 양도인에게 복귀된다.

예시: If a grantor conveys property "to A for life." 이 양도의 경우 양도인은 복귀권을 보유하게 된다. A가 사망하면, 재산은 제3자에게 양도될 권리가 지정되지 않았으므로 자동으로 양도인이나 양도인의 상속인에게 복귀된다.

2. 복귀가능권(Possibility of Reverter)

A possibility of reverter is the future interest retained by the grantor when they convey a fee simple determinable. If the specified condition occurs, the estate automatically reverts to the grantor. No legal action or re-entry by the grantor is required to reclaim the property.

Example: O conveys Blackacre "to A, so long as it is used for a school." If the property ceases to be used as a school, it automatically reverts to O.

복귀가능권(possibility of reverter)은 양도인이 조건부 단순 소유권(fee simple determinable)을 양도할 때 보유하는 미래의 권리다. 명시된 조건이 발생하면 소유권은 자동으로 양도인에게 복귀되며, 양도인이 재산을 회수하기 위해 별도의 법적 조치나 재진입을 할 필요가 없다.

예시: O conveys Blackacre "to A, so long as it is used for a school." 양도인은 복귀가능권을 보유하게 되며, 재산이 더 이상 학교로 사용되지 않으면 자동으로 O에게 복귀된다.

3. 진입권(Right of Entry)

A right of entry (also called right of reentry or power of termination) is a future interest retained by the grantor after conveying a fee simple subject to condition subsequent. The grantor must take affirmative action (such as filing a lawsuit or issuing a notice to the grantee) to reclaim the property if the condition is violated.

If the grantor fails to take action within a reasonable period, the right of reentry could be considered waived, and the grantee might continue to possess and own the property.

Example: O conveys Blackacre "to A, but if alcohol is ever sold on the property, O may reenter and reclaim the property." If A sells alcohol on the premises, the grantor (or the grantor's heirs) has the right to reclaim Blackacre, meaning O can take affirmative action to reclaim the property. However, Bob's estate continues until the grantor exercises this right.

진입권(right of entry)은 양도인이 해제조건부 단순 소유권(fee simple subject to condition subsequent)을 양도한 후 보유하는 미래의 권리다. 조건이 위반되면, 양도인은 재산을 회수하기 위해 소송을 제기하거나 양수인에게 통지를 발송하는 등의 적극적인 조치를 취해야 한다.

양도인이 합리적인 기간 내에 조치를 취하지 않으면, 진입권이 포기된 것으로 간주될 수 있으며, 양수인은 재산을 계속해서 점유하고 소유할 수 있다.

예시: O conveys Blackacre "to A, but if alcohol is ever sold on the property, O may reenter and reclaim the property." A가 해당 재산에서 술을 판매하면 양도인 O 또는 그의 상속인은 토지를 회수할 수가 있다. 그러나 O가 이 권리를 행사할 때까지 A의 소유권은 지속된다.

4. 잔여권(Remainder)

A remainder is a future interest in property created in a grantee that becomes possessory upon the expiration of a prior possessory estate, such as a life estate or an estate for years. The remainder must be created in the same conveyance that establishes the prior estate. A remainder can be vested or contingent, depending on whether the grantee is ascertainable and whether any conditions must be fulfilled before the grantee can take possession.

잔여권(remainder)은 종신소유권이나 확정기한부 소유권과 같은 선행하는 점유적 권리가 종료된 후 양수인에게 점유가 부여되는 미래의 권리다. 잔여권은 반드시 선행소유권을 설정하는 동일한 양도 문서에서 성립되어야 한다. 잔여권은 양수인이 확정되어 있는지, 양수인이 점유권을 획득하기 전에 충족되어야 할 조건이 있는지에 따라 확정잔여권(vested remainder) 또는 조건부잔여권(contingent remainder)으로 구분된다.

1) 확정잔여권(Vested Remainder)

A vested remainder is a future interest in property that is created in an ascertainable grantee and is not subject to any condition precedent other than the natural expiration of the preceding estate, meaning the person is certain to receive the interest when the prior estate ends (such as a life estate). Vested remainders can come in several forms, each with its own characteristics.

a) Indefeasibly Vested Remainder

An indefeasibly vested remainder is a remainder that is certain to become possessory in the future without any further conditions. The holder of this remainder is guaranteed to receive the property when the preceding estate ends.

Example: O conveys Blackacre "to A for life, then to B." A has a life estate, and B has an indefeasibly vested remainder. When A dies, B automatically gets full possession of the property without any conditions.

b) Vested Remainder Subject to Complete Defeasance

A vested remainder subject to complete defeasance (or a vested remainder subject to divestment) means that while the remainder is vested, the occurrence of a condition subsequent could divest the remainder interest after it has vested. In other words, the interest is vested, but there is a condition that could entirely eliminate the grantee's interest in the future.

Example: O conveys Blackacre "to A for life, then to B, but if B dies without children, then to C." B has a vested remainder, but if B dies without children, B's interest is divested, and the property will go to C.

c) Vested Remainder Subject to Open

A vested remainder subject to open is a remainder that is given to a class of people, where at least one member of the class has a vested interest. However, the number of class members who will ultimately share the interest is not fixed and can increase, meaning the property interest may be divided among more individuals as the class expands. This type of remainder is subject to potential partial reduction (diminution) if additional members of the class become entitled to share the remainder.

Once a class closes, any person who might have become a class member cannot claim an interest in the property as a class member. However, those already in gestation upon closing are included in the class.

Gestation Exception: A child conceived but not yet born when the class closes is still considered part of the class.

Rule of Convenience: Absent a closing date, this rule closes the class when any member of the class becomes entitled to immediate possession of the property, even if the grant does not specify a closing date.

Example: O conveys Blackacre "to my children." O has one child, A, at the time of conveyance. A has a vested remainder subject to open, as A's interest is vested, but the class (O's children) remains open and could include additional children if O has more children in the future.

확정잔여권(vested remainder)은 조건 없이 특정 양수인에게 부여된 미래의 권리로, 선행 소유권(예: 종신소유권)이 자연스럽게 종료되면 확실히 그 권리를 취득하게 된다. 확정잔여권에는 여러 형태가 있으며, 각기 다른 특징을 가진다.

a) 완전 확정잔여권(Indefeasibly Vested Remainder)

완전 확정잔여권은 어떠한 추가 조건 없이 미래에 확실히 점유권을 가지게 되는 잔여권이다. 완전 확정잔여권자는 선행 소유권이 종료되면 확실하게 재산을 취득하게 된다.

예시: O conveys Blackacre "to A for life, then to B." A는 종신소유권을 가지며 B는 완전 확정잔여권을 가진다. A가 사망하면 B는 자동으로 조건 없이 재산의 점유권을 가지게 된다.

b) 조건부 확정잔여권
(Vested Remainder Subject to Complete Defeasance)

조건부 확정잔여권은 잔여권이 확정되었지만, 해제조건이 발생하면 잔여권이 박탈될 수 있는 잔여권이다. 즉, 잔여권은 확정되었지만, 미래에 발생할 수 있는 조건에 따라 잔여권자가 그 권리를 상실할 수 있다.

예시: O conveys Blackacre "to A for life, then to B, but if B dies without children, then to C." B는 확정잔여권을 가지지만, B가 자녀 없이 사망하면 B의 잔여권은 박탈되고 재산은 C에게 이전된다.

c) 열림형 확정잔여권(Vested Remainder Subject to Open)

열림형 확정잔여권은 특정한 집단에 부여된 잔여권으로, 해당 집단의 구성원 중 최소 한 명이 확정된 권리를 가지고 있지만, 집단 구성원이 추가될 수 있어 이익이 나눠질 수 있다. 집단의 규모가 확정되지 않았기 때문에, 새로운 구성원이 추가되면 이익이 더 많은 사람들과 나눠질 수 있다.

집단이 닫히면 추가적인 구성원은 그 집단의 일원으로서 재산에 대한 권리를 주장할 수 없다. 그러나 집단이 닫히는 시점에 태어나지 않았지만 이미 임신 중인 자는 집단에 포함이 되는 것으로 간주된다.

임신 예외(Gestation Exception): 집단이 닫히는 시기에 출생하지 않았지만 임신 중인 아이는 집단의 일원으로 간주된다.

편리성 원칙(Rule of Convenience): 집단이 닫히는 시기가 정해지지 않은 경우, 편리성 원칙에 따라 집단의 어느 구성원이 재산에 대한 점유권을 가질 때 집단은 닫히게 되어 더 이상 구성원이 추가되지 않게 된다.

예시: O conveys Blackacre "to my children." 양도 시점에 O에게는 자녀 A가 있다. A는 열림형 확정잔여권을 가지며, A의 권리는 확정되었으나, O가 더 많은 자녀를 가지면 이 집단에 추가되며, A의 이익은 다른 자녀들과 나눠질 수 있다.

2) 조건부 잔여권(Contingent Remainder)

a) 조건부 잔여권의 유형(Types of contingent remainder)

A contingent remainder is a future interest in property that is contingent because it is either given to an unascertainable person or made subject to a condition precedent that must be fulfilled before the interest can become possessory.

i) Unascertainable Beneficiary

The future interest is contingent if the identity of the remainderman (beneficiary) is unknown or unascertainable at the time of the conveyance. The property cannot vest in someone whose identity is unknown.

Example: A conveys "to B for life, remainder to C's heirs." If C is still alive at the time of the conveyance, the remainder is contingent because C's heirs are unascertainable while C is alive (C's heirs will only be known when C dies).

ii) Condition Precedent

The remainder is contingent if it is subject to a condition precedent, which means that some condition must be met before the remainderman can take possession of the property. The condition must be fulfilled before the property can vest in the beneficiary.

Example: A conveys "to B for life, then to D if D graduates from law school." D's remainder is contingent because it is subject to the condition that D must graduate from law school before the remainder can vest.

조건부 잔여권(contingent remainder)은 잔여권자가 확정되지 않았거나, 잔여권이 점유로 전환되기 전에 충족되어야 할 정지조건이 있는 경우에 발생하는 미래의 권리다.

i) 불확정 수익자(Unascertainable Beneficiary)

잔여권자의 신원이 양도 시점에 불명확하거나 불확정인 경우, 미래의 권리는 조건부이다. 잔여권은 신원이 불확정된 사람에게는 부여될 수 없다.

예시: A conveys "to B for life, remainder to C's heirs." A가 B에게 재산을 양도하는 시점에 C가 생존해 있다면 잔여권은 조건부이다. 이는 C의 상속인이 C가 사망하기 전에는 확정될 수 없기 때문이다.

ii) 정지조건(Condition Precedent)

잔여권이 정지조건에 종속될 경우, 수익자가 재산을 점유하기 전에 반드시 충족되어야 하는 조건이 있는 것이다. 이 조건이 충족되어야 잔여권이 수익자에게 귀속될 수 있다.

예시: A conveys "to B for life, then to D if D graduates from law school." D의 잔여권은 조건부이다. D가 로스쿨을 졸업해야만 잔여권이 확정되고 점유권이 D에게 이전될 수 있기 때문이다.

b) 조건부 잔여권의 소멸 원칙 (Rule of Destructibility of Contingent Remainders)

The Rule of Destructibility of Contingent Remainders was a common law rule stating that a contingent remainder would be destroyed if it did not vest by the time the preceding estate ended. If the contingent remainder did not vest (because a condition had not yet been met or the beneficiary was unascertainable), the interest was considered void, and the grantor or their heirs would take the property in fee simple absolute.

However, in most jurisdictions today, the rule has been abolished, and contingent remainders are preserved even if they have not vested when the preceding estate terminates. The grantor retains possession (through reversion) until the condition is met, at which point the holder of the contingent remainder can take possession through a springing executory interest.

Example: O conveys Blackacre "to A for life, and if B has reached the age of 25, to B." Under the rule of destructibility, if A dies while B is still under 25, B's contingent remainder would be destroyed, and O would take the property in fee simple absolute.

Under modern law, if A dies when B is still 22, the property reverts to O in fee simple until B turns 25. B's interest is not destroyed but becomes a springing executory interest, meaning B will take possession once the condition (turning 25) is met.

조건부 잔여권의 소멸 원칙(rule of destructibility of contingent remainders)은 전통적인 보통법 원칙으로, 조건부 잔여권이 선행 소유권이 종료될 때까지 확정되지 않으면 그 잔여권이 소멸된다는 원칙이다. 만약 조건부 잔여권이 확정되지 않았다면(조건이 충족되지 않았거나 수익자가 불확정된 경우), 그 권리는 무효로 간주되어 재산은 양도인이나 그의 상속인에게 절대적 단순 소유권(fee simple absolute)으로 귀속된다.

그러나 오늘날 대부분의 관할권에서는 이 원칙이 폐지되었고, 조건부 잔여권이 선행 소유권이 종료될 때까지 확정되지 않더라도 보존된다. 이 경우, 조건이 충족될 때까지 재산은 양도인에게 복귀(reversion)되며, 조건이 충족되면 조건부 잔여권자는 도약적 미확정 권리(springing executory interest)을 통해 재산을 점유할 수 있다.

예시: O conveys Blackacre "to A for life, and if B has reached the age of 25, to B." 전통적 소멸 원칙에 따르면 A가 사망할 때 B가 아직 25세가 되지 않았다면 B의 조건부 잔여권은 소멸되고, O는 절대적 단순 소유권을 회복하게 된다. 그러나 현대법에서는 A가 사망할 때 B가 22세라면 재산은 O에게 일시적으로 복귀되지만, B의 권리는 소멸되지 않고 도약적 미확정 권리로 전환되어 B가 25세가 되면 재산을 다시 점유하게 된다.

c) 셸리 사건의 원칙(Rule in Shelley's Case)

The Rule in Shelley's Case was a common law doctrine that prevented the creation of contingent remainders in a grantee's heirs. If a grantor tried to convey a life estate to a grantee and a remainder to that grantee's heirs, the rule would automatically merge the life estate and the remainder into a fee simple absolute in the grantee. The rule applied automatically, without regard to the grantor's intent, overriding any language in the deed that might have attempted to create a remainder for the heirs.

Most jurisdictions have now abolished the Rule in Shelley's Case, and courts now honor the grantor's intent to create separate interests in the grantee and the grantee's heirs.

Example: O conveys "to A for life, remainder to A's heirs." Under the Rule in Shelley's Case, the conveyance would be treated as if O had granted A a fee simple absolute. A's life estate and the remainder to A's heirs would merge, and A would own the property outright. Under modern law, in jurisdictions where the rule has been abolished, A would receive a life estate, and A's heirs would have a contingent remainder.

셸리 사건의 원칙(rule in shelley's case)은 보통법상의 원칙으로, 양수인의 상속인에게 조건부 잔여권을 설정하는 것을 방지하는 원칙이다. 만약 양도인이 종신소유권을 양수인에게 그리고 잔여권을 그 양수인의 상속인에게 양도하려고 시도할 경우, 이 원칙에 의해 종신소유권과 잔여권은 자동으로 통합되어 양수인에게 절대적 단순 소유권(fee simple absolute)이 부여된다. 이 원칙은 양도인의 의도와 관계없이 자동으로 적용되며, 양수인의 상속인에게 잔여권을 설정하려는 문구를 무효화한다.

현재 대부분의 관할권에서는 셸리 사건의 원칙이 폐지되었으며, 법원은 이제 양수인과 양수인의 상속인에게 별도의 권리를 부여하려는 양도인의 의도를 존중한다.

예시: O conveys "to A for life, remainder to A's heirs." 셸리 사건의 원칙하에서는 이 양도가 A에게 절대적 단순 소유권을 부여한 것으로 간주되며, A의 종신소유권과 A의 상속인에게 주어진 잔여권이 통합되어 A가 재산을 완전히 소유하게 된다. 그러나 현대법에서 이 원칙이 폐지된 관할권에서는 A는 종신소유권을 갖고, A의 상속인은 조건부 잔여권을 가지게 된다.

d) 가치있는 소유권 원칙(Doctrine of Worthier Title)

> The Doctrine of Worthier Title prevents the creation of remainders in the grantor's heirs, presuming that the grantor intended the property to revert back to them, rather than pass to their heirs through a remainder.
>
> The Doctrine of Worthier Title is a rule of construction, not a rule of law like the Rule in Shelley's Case. As a rule of construction, it is based on an assumption about the grantor's intent, but it can be rebutted by clear evidence that the grantor intended to create a remainder in their heirs. If the grantor's intent to give a remainder to their heirs is explicit, then the doctrine does not apply.
>
> The Doctrine of Worthier Title has not been abolished in all jurisdictions and is still viable in some states today.
>
> Example: O conveys Blackacre "to A for life, then to O's heirs." Under the Doctrine of Worthier Title, the remainder in O's heirs would be void, and the property would revert back to O upon A's death. A has a life estate, and O retains a reversion. Without the Doctrine of Worthier Title, A has a life estate, and O's heirs have a contingent remainder (because O is still alive, and thus, O's heirs are unascertainable until O's death)

가치있는 소유권 원칙(doctrine of worthier title)은 양도인의 상속인에게 잔여권을 설정하는 것을 방지하는 원칙으로, 양도인이 재산을 상속인에게 잔여권으로 넘기려는 것보다는 양도인 자신에게 재산을 복귀시키려는 의도를 가졌다고 추정하는 것이다.

가치있는 소유권 원칙은 셸리 사건의 원칙과 달리 법률적 원칙이 아닌 의제 원칙이다. 즉, 이 법리는 양도인의 의도에 대한 추정을 기반으로 하지만, 양도인이 상속인에게 잔여권을 설정하려는 명확한 의도를 표현하면 이 추정은 반박될 수 있다. 따라서, 양도인이 상속인에게 잔여권을 부여하려는 명시적인 의도가 있으면 이 원칙이 적용되지 않는다.

가치있는 소유권 원칙은 모든 관할권에서 폐지된 것은 아니며, 일부 주에서는 여전히 유효하다.

예시: O conveys Blackacre "to A for life, then to O's heirs." 가치있는 소유권 원칙에 따르면 O의 상속인에게 부여된 잔여권은 무효가 되며, A가 사망하면 재산은 O에게 복귀된다. A는 종신소유권을 가지고, O는 복귀권을 보유하게 된다. 이 원칙이 적용되지 않는 경우에는 A가 종신소유권을 가지고, O의 상속인은 조건부 잔여권을 가지게 된다(왜냐하면 O가 생존해 있는 동안에는 O의 상속인이 확정되지 않기 때문이다).

5. 미확정 권리(Executory Interests)

An executory interest is a type of future interest in property held by a third party that does not follow the natural expiration of a prior estate, as a remainder does, but instead cuts short the preceding estate upon the occurrence of a specified condition.

The two types of executory interests are shifting executory interest and springing executory interest.

미확정 권리(executory interest)은 선행 소유권의 자연스러운 종료를 따르는 잔여권과 달리, 특정 조건이 발생하면 선행 소유권을 단축시키고 제3자가 소유권을 취득하는 미래의 권리다.

미확정 권리에는 이전적 미확정 권리(shifting executory interest)과 도약적 미확정 권리(springing executory interest)이 있다.

1) 이전적 미확정 권리(Shifting Executory Interest)

A shifting executory interest divests the interest of a prior grantee upon the occurrence of a specified condition. In this case, the property "shifts" from one grantee to another.

Example: A conveys Blackacre "to B and his heirs, but if C returns from London, then to C." In this scenario, B holds a fee simple subject to an executory limitation, and C holds a shifting executory interest. If C returns from London, C's interest will divest B's estate, and C will take ownership of Blackacre.

이전적 미확정 권리(Shifting Executory Interest)은 특정 조건이 발생하면 선행 양수인의 권리를 박탈하고 재산이 다른 제3자에게 이전되는 경우를 의미한다. 즉, 재산이 한 양수인에서 다른 양수인으로 이전되는 것이다.

예시: A conveys Blackacre "to B and his heirs, but if C returns from London, then to C." B는 제3자 이전 조건부 단순 소유권(fee simple subject to an executory interest or fee simple subject to an executory limitation)을 가지며, C는 이전적 미확정 권리(shifting executory interest)을 가진다. 만약 C가 런던에서 돌아오면, B의 소유권은 박탈되고, C가 토지의 소유권을 취득하게 된다.

2) 도약적 미확정 권리(Springing Executory Interest)

A springing executory interest divests the interest of the grantor or fills a gap in possession, often when the estate temporarily reverts to the grantor. The springing executory interest "springs" into effect, usually after a gap or delay.

Example: A conveys Blackacre "to B for life, and two years after B's death, to C and his heirs." Here, A retains a two-year reversion after B's death, and C holds a springing executory interest. C's interest springs into effect two years after B's death, divesting A's temporary reversion.

도약적 미확정 권리(Springing Executory Interest)은 양도인의 권리를 박탈하거나 점유권의 공백을 메우며, 일반적으로 재산이 일시적으로 양도인에게 복귀된 후 발생한다. 도약적 미확정 권리는 시간적 공백이나 지연 후에 제3자가 소유권을 취득하게 된다.

예시: A conveys Blackacre "to B for life, and two years after B's death, to C and his heirs." A는 B가 사망한 후 2년 동안 복귀권을 보유하고, C는 도약적 미확정 권리를 가진다. B가 사망한 후 2년이 지나면, C의 권리가 발효되어 A의 임시적인 복귀권을 박탈되고 C가 소유권을 취득하게 된다.

6. 영구불확정금지 원칙(Rule Against Perpetuities)

The Rule Against Perpetuities (RAP) is a legal principle designed to prevent the indefinite delay of property ownership vesting. Under the Rule, certain future interests are valid only if they are guaranteed to either vest or fail to vest no later than 21 years after the death of a relevant "life in being" (measuring life) at the time the interest is created. The goal of RAP is to prevent property from being tied up indefinitely by future interests.

영구불확정금지 원칙(rule against perpetuities, RAP)은 재산권의 확정이 무기한 지연되는 것을 방지하기 위한 법적 원칙이다. 이 원칙에 따르면, 일정한 미래의 권리는 해당 권리가 성립될 당시 생존하고 있는 관련 인물(life in being)의 사망, 즉 기준생애(measuring life)의 종료 후 21년 이내에 확정되거나 확정되지 않는 것이 확실하게 되어야 유효하다. 영구불확정금지 원칙의 목적은 재산이 미래의 권리로 인해 무기한 묶이는 것을 방지하는 데 있다.

1) 일반원칙(General rule)

a) Measuring Life and 21 Years

The Rule applies to future interests and requires that they must vest, if at all, no later than 21 years after the death of a relevant life in being at the time the interest is created. A life in being is any person alive at the time the interest is created and directly relevant to the property interest vesting.

b) Vesting or Failing

To satisfy the Rule, it must be clear that the future interest will either vest or fail (become certain or fail to become certain) within the time limit (the lifetime of a relevant person plus 21 years).

c) Example Violating RAP

A conveys Blackacre "to B for life, and then to the first male descendant of B, then to C." This conveyance violates the Rule, because it may be many generations before a male descendant of B is born (if at all), which could exceed the RAP time period. The interest might not vest within 21 years of the death of any relevant life in being.

d) Example Satisfying RAP

A conveys Blackacre "to B for life, and then to B's first son who reaches the age of 18, then to C." This is valid under the Rule, because any son of B will either reach the age of 18 within 21 years of B's death or will not (vest or fail). Since the condition is tied to a life in being (B), the interest will either vest or fail within 21 years after B's death.

e) Affected future interests

RAP applies only to the following interests: contingent remainders, vested remainders subject to open, executory interests, powers of appointment, rights of first refusal, and options.

It does not apply to future interests that revert to the grantor (i.e., reversion, possibility of reverter, right of reentry).

a) 기준생애와 21년(Measuring Life and 21 Years)

영구불확정금지 원칙은 미래의 권리에 적용되며, 권리가 확정되려면 그 권리가 성립될 당시의 관련 인물이 사망한 후 21년 이내에 확정되거나 확정되지 않아야 한다. 관련 인물은 권리가 성립된 시점에 살아 있는 자로, 해당 재산 권리의 확정과 직접적으로 관련이 있는 자이다.

b) 확정 또는 소멸(Vesting or Failing)

영구불확정금지 원칙을 충족하기 위해서는, 미래의 권리가 해당 기간 내에 확정되거나 또는 확정되지 않는 것이 명확해야 한다. 즉, 관련 인물의 생존 기간과 사망 후 21년 이내에 미래의 권리가 확정되거나 소멸해야 한다.

c) RAP를 위반하는 예시(Example Violating RAP)

A conveys Blackacre "to B for life, and then to the first male descendant of B, then to C." 이 양도는 RAP를 위반한다. 왜냐하면 B의 남성 후손이 몇 세대 이후에 태어날지(혹은 태어나지 않을지) 알 수 없기 때문에, 이는 RAP의 기간 제한인 21년을 초과할 수 있다. 이 권리는 관련 인물의 사망 후 21년 이내에 확정되지 않을 수 있다.

d) RAP를 충족하는 예시(Example Satisfying RAP)

A conveys Blackacre "to B for life, and then to B's first son who reaches the age of 18, then to C." 이 양도는 RAP를 충족한다. B의 첫 번째 아들이 18세가 되는 조건은 B의 생존기간에 따라 결정되므로, B가 사망한 후 21년 이내에 아들이 18세에 도달하거나 도달하지 않게 되어 권리가 확정되거나 소멸하게 된다.

e) RAP이 적용되는 미래의 권리(Affected Future Interests)

RAP는 다음과 같은 미래의 권리에만 적용된다. 즉, 조건부 잔여권(contingent remainders), 열림형 확정잔여권(vested remainder subject to open), 미확정 권리(executory interests), 지정권(powers of appointment), 우선매수권(rights of first refusal), 옵션(options)에

RAP가 적용된다.

RAP는 양도인에게 복귀하는 미래의 권리에는 적용되지 않는다. 예를 들어, 복귀권(reversion), 복귀가능권(possibility of reverter), 진입권(right of entry)과 같은 권리에는 RAP가 적용되지 않는다.

2) 기준생애(Measuring Life)

A measuring life must be a human life, and the rule is concerned with the lifetime of a person whose life is directly related to the vesting of the future interest.

Example: O conveys Blackacre "to A for life, and then to A's children who reach the age of 22." A's life is the measuring life, and the RAP period is 21 years after A's death. The future interest must vest or fail (the children reaching age 22) within this period to satisfy RAP.

If no measuring life is specified, the rule requires that the interest vests or fails within 21 years of its creation.

Example: O conveys Blackacre "to a charity for as long as the property is used as a children's playground, and then to B." Since there is no measuring life (because the condition is based on the use of the property), B's interest must vest or fail within 21 years of its creation. However, there is no guarantee when or if the property will stop being used as a playground, making B's interest void under RAP.

기준생애는 반드시 사람의 생애이어야 하며, 영구불확정금지 원칙은 미래의 권리의 확정과 직접적으로 관련된 사람의 생애에 초점을 맞춘다.

예시: O conveys Blackacre "to A for life, and then to A's children who reach the age of 22." A의 생명이 기준생애가 된다. RAP의 기간은 A가 사망한 후 21년이며, 이 기간 내에 A의 자녀들이 22세에 도달하거나 도달하지 않는 것이 확정되어야 한다.

기준생애가 지정되지 않은 경우, 영구불확정금지 원칙에 따라 미래의 권리는 그 성립 시점으로부터 21년 이내에 확정되거나 소멸되어야 한다.

예시: O conveys Blackacre "to a charity for as long as the property is used as a children's playground, and then to B." 이 조건은 부동산의 사용에 기반하므로 기준생애가 특정되어 있지 않다. 따라서 B의 미래의 권리는 성립 시점으로부터 21년 이내에 확정되거나 소멸되어야 한다. 그러나 언제 재산이 더 이상 놀이터로 사용되지 않을지 보장될 수 없으므로, B의 미래의 권리는 RAP에 의해 무효가 된다.

3) 확정 또는 미확정 요건(Vest or Fail Requirement)

The RAP requires that the future interest must either vest or fail to vest within the applicable time period. If there is any possibility that the interest could vest after the life in being plus 21 years, it violates RAP.

영구불확정금지 원칙은 미래의 권리가 해당 기간 내에 확정되거나(vest) 미확정(fail to vest) 될 것을 요구한다. 만약 그 미래의 권리가 기준생애의 기간이 소멸한 후 21년이 지난 시점에서 확정될 가능성이 조금이라도 있다면, 이는 RAP를 위반하게 된다.

4) 집단에 대한 양도의 특별 원칙(Special Rule for Transfers to a Class)

Under RAP, if a future interest is transferred to a class of people (e.g., children or grandchildren), and the interest violates RAP for any member of the class, the entire class gift is void ("bad as to one, bad as to all"). To be valid, it must be certain that all class members' interests will vest within the perpetuity period.

Example: O devises Blackacre "to A for life, and then to A's children who graduate from college." At the time of O's death, A has two children: X (who has graduated) and Y (who has not). X has a vested remainder subject to open, and Y has a contingent remainder. If A later has another child, Z, who takes more than 21 years to graduate from college, Z's interest violates RAP. As a result, the interests of all of A's children (X, Y, and Z) are void.

RAP는 미래의 권리가 한 집단(예: 자녀 또는 손자)에게 양도될 때, 그 집단의 한 구성원이 RAP를 위반하면 그 집단 전체에 대한 양도가 무효가 된다는 원칙을 적용한다. RAP을 위반하지 않고 유효하려면, 집단의 모든 구성원의 미래의 권리가 RAP의 기간 내에 확정될 것이 확실해야 한다.

예시: O devises Blackacre "to A for life, and then to A's children who graduate from college." O가 사망할 때 A에게는 이미 대학을 졸업한 자녀 X와 아직 졸업하지 않은 자녀 Y가 있다. X는 열림형 확정 잔여권(vested remainder subject to open)을 가지고, y는 조건부 잔여권(contingent remainder)을 가진다. 만약 A가 이후 자녀 Z를 낳았고, Z가 21년 이상 대학을 졸업하지 않는다면, Z의 권리는 RAP를 위반하게 된다. 그 결과, A의 모든 자녀들(X, Y, Z)의 미래의 권리가 무효가 된다.

5) RAP의 특별 원칙(Special RAP Rules)

a) Fertile Octogenarian

For the purposes of RAP, anyone - even an 80-year-old woman - can be considered capable of having children.

Example: O conveys Blackacre "to A for life, then to A's children who reach the age of 30." A is 80 years old, with one child, X, who is 35. X has a vested remainder subject to open, as A is presumed capable of having more children. Since A could have another child who may not reach 30 until more than 21 years after A's death, X's interest is void under the "bad as to one, bad as to all" rule.

b) Charity-to-Charity Exception

Transfers between two charitable organizations are exempt from RAP. The rule does not apply to charity-to-charity transfers, meaning that future interests between charities can extend beyond the RAP period.

Example: Blackacre is conveyed "to charity A, so long as the premises are used for a school, and then to charity B." Although charity B's interest might not vest within the RAP period, it is valid because the charity-to-charity exception applies.

a) 80대 가임 원칙(Fertile Octogenarian)

RAP 적용을 위해, 나이에 관계없이 누구나, 심지어 80대의 여성이더라도, 자녀를 가질 수 있는 것으로 간주된다.

예시: O conveys Blackacre "to A for life, then to A's children who reach the age of 30." A는 80세로, 자녀 X는 35세이다. X는 열림형 확정 잔여권(vested remainder subject to open)을 가지고 있다. RAP는 A가 더 많은 자녀를 가질 수 있다고 가정하므로, A가 이후에 자녀를 낳아 그 자녀가 30세에 도달하는 것이 A의 사망 후 21년을 초과할 수 있다. 따라서 X의 권리는 "한 명이 위반하면 모두 무효" 원칙에 따라 무효가 된다.

b) 자선단체 간 양도 예외(Charity-to-Charity Exception)

두 자선단체 간의 양도는 RAP에서 면제된다. 자선단체 간의 양도는 RAP가 적용되지 않으며, 자선단체 간의 미래의 권리는 RAP 기간을 초과해도 유효하다.

예시: Blackacre is conveyed "to charity A, so long as the premises are used for a school, and then to charity B." 자선단체 B의 권리가 RAP 기간 내에 확정되지 않더라도, 자선단체 간의 예외가 적용되므로 유효하다.

6) RAP의 현대적 개혁(RAP Modern Reforms)

a) Wait and See Doctrine

Many states have adopted the Uniform Statutory Rule Against Perpetuities, which follows a "wait and see" approach. Instead of voiding interests immediately, courts will wait to see if the interest actually vests within 90 years.

Example: O conveys Blackacre "to A for life, then to A's first grandchild to reach the age of 25." At the time of the conveyance, A has no grandchildren. Under the traditional Rule Against Perpetuities, this interest could be void because it might not vest within 21 years after the death of A (since A could have grandchildren born more than 21 years after their death). Instead of voiding the interest immediately, the court would "wait and see" whether A's grandchild reaches the age of 25 within the vesting period (which could be 90 years under USRAP). If a grandchild does reach 25 within that period, the interest is valid. If not, the interest is voided.

b) Cy Pres Doctrine

Some states allow courts to reform a conveyance under the cy pres doctrine, which means the court will modify the terms of the conveyance to comply with RAP while staying as close as possible to the transferor's intent.

Example: O conveys Blackacre "to A for life, and then to A's grandchildren who reach the age of 30." This provision violates RAP because A could have grandchildren who do not reach the age of 30 until more than 21 years after A's death. A court might apply the Cy Pres Doctrine by reforming the conveyance to read "to A's grandchildren who reach the age of 21," rather than 30. This adjustment ensures that the interest vests within the permissible RAP period.

a) 관망 원칙(Wait and See Doctrine)

많은 주에서는 통일 영구불확정금지 규정(Uniform Statutory Rule Against Perpetuities)을 채택하여 "관망(wait and see)" 접근 방식을 따르고 있다. 이 원칙에 따라 미래의 권리가 즉시 무효화되지 않고, 해당 권리가 실제로 90년 이내에 확정되는지 여부를 기다려 보는 것이다.

예시: O conveys Blackacre "to A for life, then to A's first grandchild to reach the age of 25." 양도 시점에 A는 손자가 없는 경우, 전통적인 RAP에 따르면, 이 양도에서 미래의 권리는 A가 사망한 후 21년이 지나야 손자가 태어날 가능성이 있기 때문에 무효가 될 수 있다. 그러나 "관망(wait and see)" 원칙을 따르면, 법원은 즉시 미래의 권리를 무효화하지 않고, A의 손자가 25세에 도달하는지 지켜본다(USRAP 하에서는 그 기간이 90년이 될 수 있다). 만약 손자가 해당 기간 내에 25세에 도달하면 미래의 권리는 유효하고, 그렇지 않으면 그 권리는 무효가 된다.

b) 근접 원칙(Cy Pres Doctrine)

일부 주에서는 법원이 근접 원칙에 따라 양도의 조건을 수정할 수 있도록 허용한다. 이는 양도인의 의도에 최대한 가깝게 유지하면서도 RAP에 부합하도록 양도 조건을 조정하는 것이다.

예시: O conveys Blackacre "to A for life, and then to A's grandchildren who reach the age of 30." A가 사망한 후 21년 이상이 되어도 손자가 30세에 도달할 수 없을 수도 있으므로 이 양도는 RAP를 위반하게 된다. 법원은 근접 원칙을 적용해 이 양도를 "to A's grandchildren who reach the age of 21"로 수정할 수 있다. 이 수정은 미래의 권리가 RAP의 허용 기간 내에 확정되도록 보장하게 된다.

C 공동 소유권(Concurrent Estates)

Concurrent estates (or co-tenancy) refer to the simultaneous ownership of real property by two or more individuals. The three primary forms of concurrent estates are joint tenancy, tenancy in common, and tenancy by the entirety.

공동 소유권(concurrent estates 또는 co-tenancy)은 두 명 이상의 개인이 동시에 부동산을 소유하는 것을 의미한다. 공동 소유권은 공동 연대 소유권(joint tenancy), 공동 지분 소유권(tenancy in common) 및 부부 공동 소유권(tenancy by the entirety)이 있다.

1. 공동 연대 소유권(Joint Tenancy)

A joint tenancy is a form of concurrent ownership where two or more individuals own property with the right of survivorship. Upon the death of one joint tenant, their interest automatically passes to the surviving joint tenants.

1) Right of Survivorship

The distinguishing feature of a joint tenancy. When one joint tenant dies, their interest passes to the surviving joint tenants automatically.

Example: A, B, and C own a house as joint tenants. If A dies, B and C automatically inherit A's share, and the property is now owned equally by B and C.

2) Four Unities (PITT)

To create a valid joint tenancy, four unities must be present:

a) Unity of Possession: Equal right to possess the whole property.

b) Unity of Interest: Equal interest in the property.

c) Unity of Time: The interests must be acquired at the same time.

d) Unity of Title: The interests must be acquired through the same legal document (deed, will, etc.).

3) Severance of Joint Tenancy

Joint tenancies can be severed, converting the ownership into a tenancy in common. Severance can occur in several ways, such as a lifetime transfer (inter vivos), mortgage (in some jurisdictions), or judicial lien.

a) Severance by Conveyance

i) Lifetime Transfer (Inter Vivos): A joint tenant can sever the joint tenancy by transferring their interest during their lifetime. The transfer converts the joint tenancy into a tenancy in common.

Example: X, Y, and Z hold Greenacre as joint tenants. X transfers her interest to C during her lifetime. Now, X's interest is severed, and C holds a one-third interest as a tenant in common, while Y and Z remain joint tenants with each other.

ii) At Death (No Severance): A joint tenant cannot devise their interest in a will. Upon their death, the property passes to the surviving joint tenants by right of survivorship, overriding any will.

b) Severance by Mortgage

i) Lien Theory (Majority Rule): In lien theory states, a mortgage is considered a lien on the property and does not sever the joint tenancy unless there is a foreclosure sale.

ii) Title Theory (Minority Rule): In title theory states, a mortgage is considered a transfer of title, which severs the joint tenancy.

c) Other Forms of Severance

i) Judicial Lien: A lien placed on a joint tenant's interest generally does not sever the joint tenancy unless the property is sold in foreclosure.

i) Leases: There is a split among jurisdictions on whether leasing an interest severs the joint tenancy. Some courts hold that it severs the joint tenancy, while others view the lease as suspending the joint tenancy until the lease expires.

iii) Intentional Killings: If one joint tenant intentionally kills another, some states impose a constructive trust on the killer's interest, meaning the killer holds the property for the benefit of the deceased's estate. Other jurisdictions sever the joint tenancy upon a felonious killing.

공동 연대 소유권(joint tenancy)은 두 명 이상의 개인이 생존자 취득권(right of survivorship)을 가지며 부동산을 공동 소유하는 형태이다. 공동 연대 소유권자 중 한 명이 사망하면 그 지분은 자동으로 다른 생존한 공동 연대 소유권자들에게 이전된다.

1) 생존자 취득권(Right of Survivorship)

공동 연대 소유권의 가장 두드러진 특징은 생존자 취득권이다. 공동 연대 소유권자 중 한 명이 사망하면 그 지분은 생존한 공동 연대 소유권자들에게 자동으로 이전되며, 유언을 통해 그 지분을 양도할 수 없다.

예시: A, B, and C own a house as joint tenants. A가 사망하면 A의 지분은 자동으로 B와 C에게 이전된다. 따라서 B와 C는 이제 동일한 지분(1/2)을 갖고 집을 소유하게 된다.

2) 네 가지 통일 요건(Four Unities, PITT)

유효한 공동 연대 소유권을 만들기 위해서는 네 가지 통일 요건이 필요하다.

a) 점유의 통일(Unity of Possession): 모든 공동 연대 소유권자가 전체 재산에 대해 동등한 점유권을 가져야 한다.

b) 권리의 통일(Unity of Interest): 모든 공동 연대 소유권자가 재산에 대해 동등한 권리를 가져야 한다.

c) 시간의 통일(Unity of Time): 공동 연대 소유권자들이 동일한 시점에 권리를 취득해야 한다.

d) 소유권 증서의 통일(Unity of Title): 공동 연대 소유권자들이 동일한 법적 문서(증서, 유언 등)를 통해 권리를 취득해야 한다.

3) 공동 연대 소유권의 분리(Severance of Joint Tenancy)

공동 연대 소유권은 분리될 수 있으며, 이 경우 소유권은 공동 지분 소유권으로 전환된다. 분리는 여러 가지 방식으로 발생할 수 있다.

a) 양도에 의한 분리(Severance by Conveyance)

i) 생전 양도(Inter Vivos Transfer): 공동 연대 소유권자는 생전에 자신의 지분을 양도하여 공동 연대 소유권을 분리할 수 있다. 이 경우 소유권은 공동 지분 소유권으로 전환된다.

예시: X, Y, and Z hold Greenacre as joint tenants. X transfers her interest to C during her lifetime. X의 지분은 분리되었으며, C는 공동 지분 소유권의 소유권자로서 1/3의 지분을 가지고, Y와 Z는 서로 공동 연대 소유권을 유지한다.

ii) 사망 시(At Death): 공동 연대 소유권자는 자신의 지분을 유언으로 양도할 수 없으며, 사망 시 그 지분은 생존한 공동 연대 소유권자에게 자동으로 이전된다.

b) 저당권 설정에 의한 분리(Severance by Mortgage)

i) 담보 이론(Lien Theory, 다수의견): 담보 이론을 따르는 주에서는 저당권을 재산에 대한 채권으로 간주하며, 저당권이 공동 연대 소유권을 분리하지 않는다. 다만, 담보권 실행 경매가 되면 분리될 수 있다.

ii) 소유권 이론(Title Theory, 소수의견): 소유권 이론을 따르는 주에서는 저당권을 소유권의 양도로 간주하여 공동 연대 소유권을 분리한다.

c) 기타 분리 형태(Other Forms of Severance)

i) 사법적 담보(Judicial Lien): 공동 연대 소유권자의 지분에 대한 담보권은 일반적으로 공동 연대 소유권을 분리하지 않으나, 담보권 실행으로 재산이 매각될 경우에는 분리가 된다.

ii) 임대(Leases): 임대가 공동 연대 소유권을 분리하는지에 대해서는 관할권마다 다르다. 일부 법원은 임대가 공동 연대 소유권을 분리한다고 보고, 다른 법원은 임대가 종료될 때까지 공동 연대 소유권을 보유한다고 본다.

iii) 고의적 살인(Intentional Killings): 한 공동 연대 소유권자가 다른 공동 연대 소유권자를 고의로 살해한 경우, 일부 주에서는 살인자의 지분에 대해 의제신탁을 설정하여 그 재산이 사망자의 상속인을 위해 관리되도록 한다. 다른 관할권에서는 중범죄적 살인이 발생할 경우 공동 연대 소유권을 분리한다.

2. 공동 지분 소유권(Tenancy in Common)

A tenancy in common is the default form of co-tenancy when two or more people own property together, unless otherwise specified. Each co-tenant holds an undivided interest in the property and has the right to possess and use the whole property, regardless of the size of their individual interest.

1) Equal Right to Possession (Unity of Possession)

All tenants in common have an equal right to possess the entire property, even if they own unequal shares.

2) No Right of Survivorship

When a tenant in common dies, their interest passes to their heirs or through their will, not to the other tenants in common.

Example: A and B purchase a property together as tenants in common. A owns 60%, and B owns 40%. If A dies, A's 60% interest passes to A's heirs or as specified in A's will, not to B.

3) Freely Transferable

Each tenant in common can sell, lease, or devise (transfer by will) their interest without affecting the rights of the other tenants. A tenant in common may also lease their interest, and the other tenants are entitled to share possession with the lessee.

4) Presumption of Tenancy in Common

In most states, a conveyance to two or more people creates a tenancy in common unless the language explicitly creates a joint tenancy or tenancy by the entirety.

공동 지분 소유권(tenancy in common)은 두 명 이상의 개인이 함께 재산을 소유할 때, 다른 형태의 소유권이 명시되지 않는 한 기본적으로 적용되는 형태이다. 각 소유권자는 재산에 대해 나뉘지 않은 지분을 보유하며, 자신의 지분 비율과 관계없이 전체 재산을 사용할 권리를 가진다.

1) 점유의 통일(Unity of Possession)

모든 공유 지분 소유권자는 자신이 소유한 지분 크기에 관계없이 전체 재산에 대해 동등한 점유권을 가진다.

2) 생존자 취득권 부존재(No Right of Survivorship)

공유 지분 소유권자가 사망하면 그 지분은 다른 소유권자에게 자동으로 이전되지 않고, 그들의 상속인에게 상속되거나 유언에 따라 이전된다.

예시: A and B purchase a property together as tenants in common. A owns 60%, and B owns 40%. A가 사망하면, A의 60% 지분은 B에게 이전되지 않고 A의 상속인에게 상속되거나 A의 유언에 명시된 대로 이전된다.

공동 지분 소유권에서는 생존자 취득권이 적용되지 않기 때문에, A의 지분은 다른 공동 지분 소유권자에게 자동으로 넘어가지 않는다.

3) 자유로운 양도(Freely Transferable)

각 공동 지분 소유권자는 자신의 지분을 다른 소유권자의 권리에 영향을 미치지 않고 자유롭게 매각, 임대 또는 유증할 수 있다. 공동 지분 소유권자는 자신의 지분을 임대할 수도 있으며, 다른 소유권자들은 임차인과 함께 재산을 점유할 권리가 있다.

4) Tenancy in Common 추정(Presumption of Tenancy in Common)

대부분의 주에서는 두 명 이상의 사람에게 재산을 양도할 경우, 문서에서 명시적으로 공동 연대 소유권이나 부부 공동 소유권을 규정하지 않는 한 공동 지분 소유권이 성립되는 것으로 간주한다.

3. 부부 공동 소유권(Tenancy by the Entirety)

A tenancy by the entirety is a form of concurrent ownership that is available only to married couples. It provides each spouse with an undivided interest in the property, along with the right of survivorship.

1) Fifth Unity - Unity of Person

In addition to the four unities required for a joint tenancy, tenancy by the entirety requires the spouses to be married at the time the property is conveyed.

2) Right of Survivorship

Upon the death of one spouse, the surviving spouse automatically takes full ownership of the property.

3) No Unilateral Transfer or Encumbrance

Neither spouse can unilaterally transfer or encumber the property (e.g., through sale or mortgage) without the consent of the other spouse.

부부 공동 소유권(tenancy by the entirety)은 결혼한 부부에게만 허용되는 공동 소유권 형태로, 각 배우자가 재산에 대해 나뉘지 않은 지분을 보유하며 생존자 취득권을 가진다.

1) 다섯 번째 통일 요건 – 인적 통일(Unity of Person)

부부 공동 소유권은 기존의 공동 연대 소유권에 필요한 네 가지 통일 요건 외에도, 인적 통일 요건 즉 재산이 양도될 당시 부부 공동 소유권자는 혼인한 부부일 것을 요구한다.

2) 생존자 취득권(Right of Survivorship)

배우자 중 한 명이 사망하면 생존 배우자가 자동으로 해당 재산의 전체 소유권을 취득한다.

3) 일방적 양도 또는 담보 설정 금지(No Unilateral Transfer or Encumbrance)

배우자 중 한 명은 다른 배우자의 동의 없이 일방적으로 재산을 양도하거나 담보를 설정할 수 없다.

4. 공동 소유권자의 권리와 의무(Rights and Obligations of Co-Tenants)

In a concurrent estate, co-tenants have specific rights and obligations related to the possession, use, and management of the jointly owned property. These rights ensure that each co-tenant can enjoy the benefits of ownership while balancing the needs of their fellow co-owners.

공유 소유권(concurrent estate)에서 공동 소유권자들은 공동으로 소유한 재산의 점유, 사용, 관리에 관한 일정한 권리와 의무를 가진다. 이러한 권리는 각 공동 소유권자가 소유권의 혜택을 누릴 수 있도록 하면서, 다른 공동 소유권자의 필요를 균형 있게 고려할 수 있도록 보장하는 것이다.

1) 점유(Possession)

Equal Right to Possess: Each co-tenant has the right to possess and use the entire property, regardless of their individual share. There is no requirement for co-tenants to physically share the property unless there is an agreement to the contrary.

No Rent for Exclusive Use: Generally, a co-tenant in possession does not owe rent to the other co-tenants for their exclusive use of the property, even if the other co-tenants do not use the property.

No Sharing of Business Profits: If a co-tenant operates a business on the property, they are typically not required to share profits earned from the business with the other co-tenants.

No Adverse Possession: A co-tenant's exclusive use of the property does not, by itself, give rise to adverse possession of another co-tenant's interest.

Ouster: If a co-tenant prevents another co-tenant from accessing the property, the ousted co-tenant can bring an action for ouster to regain access and recover the value of the property's use during the time they were excluded.

Natural Resources: A co-tenant is entitled to the property's natural resources (e.g., timber, minerals, oil, gas) in proportion to their ownership share.

동등한 점유권(equal right to possess): 각 공동 소유권자는 자신의 지분과 관계없이 재산 전체를 점유하고 사용할 권리가 있다. 공동 소유권자들 간에 별도의 합의가 없는 한, 물리적으로 재산을 공유할 의무는 없다.

독점 사용에 대한 임대료 지급 의무 부존재(No Rent for Exclusive Use): 한 공동 소유권자가 재산을 독점적으로 사용하더라도, 다른 공동 소유권자에게 임대료를 지불할 의무는 없다. 이는 다른 공동 소유권자가 재산을 사용하지 않더라도 동일하게 적용된다.

사업 이익 공유 의무 부존재(No Sharing of Business Profits): 한 공동 소유권자가 부동산에서 사업을 운영하더라도, 그로 인한 이익을 다른 공동 소유권자들과 나누어야 할 의무는 없다.

점유취득시효 부존재(No Adverse Possession): 공동 소유권자가 재산을 독점적으로 사용하더라도, 그 자체로 다른 공동 소유권자의 지분에 대한 점유취득시효가 성립하지 않는다.

배제(Ouster): 공동 소유권자가 다른 공동 소유권자의 재산 접근을 막을 경우, 배제된 공동 소유권자는 배제에 대한 소송을 제기하여 접근 권리를 회복할 수 있으며, 배제된 기간 동안의 재산의 사용 가치를 회수할 수 있다.

자연 자원(Natural Resources): 공동 소유권자는 자신이 소유한 지분에 비례하여 재산의 자연 자원(예: 목재, 광물, 석유, 가스)을 사용할 권리가 있다.

2) 임대수익(Rents)

If a co-tenant rents the property to a third party, they must account to the other co-tenants for the rent received. However, they are allowed to deduct operating expenses (e.g., taxes or repairs) before dividing the net proceeds. Third-party rents are divided among the co-tenants based on each tenant's ownership interest in the property.

공동 소유권자가 재산을 제3자에게 임대하는 경우, 그 임대 수익을 다른 공동 소유권자들과 나누어야 한다. 다만, 임대 수익을 분배하기 전에 운영비(예: 세금, 수리비 등)를 공제할 수 있다. 제3자로부터 발생한 임대 수익은 각 공동 소유권자가 소유한 지분 비율에 따라 분배된다.

3) 수리(Repairs)

The majority view is that contribution for necessary repairs can be compelled in actions for accounting or partition. The repairing co-tenant have a right to contribution for reasonable repairs, provided that the repairing co-tenant has notified the others of the need for repairs.

다수의견에 따르면, 필수적인 수리에 대한 기여는 회계 청구(accounting)나 분할 청구(partition) 소송에서 강제될 수 있다. 수리를 진행한 공동 소유권자는 합리적인 수리에 대한 비용을 다른 공동 소유권자에게 청구할 권리가 있으며, 이때 수리를 진행하기 전에 다른 공동 소유권자들에게 수리 필요성을 통지해야 한다.

4) 운영비(Operating Expenses)

A co-tenant who pays more than their share of necessary or beneficial operating expenses (e.g., taxes, mortgage interest) can seek contribution from the other co-tenants, unless the paying co-tenant is in sole possession of the property. A co-tenant in sole possession can collect only for the amount that exceeds the rental value of the property.

필수적이거나 유익한 운영비(예: 세금, 저당권 이자)를 다른 공동 소유권자보다 더 많이 지불한 공동 소유권자는 다른 공동 소유권자들에게 해당 비용을 청구할 수 있다. 다만, 단독 점유 중인 공동 소유권자는 재산의 임대 가치보다 초과한 금액에 대해서만 비용을 청구할 수 있다.

5) 분할(Partition)

Both tenants in common and joint tenants have the unilateral right to seek a partition of the property. This right allows them to divide or sell the property if they no longer wish to own it jointly. Tenants by the entirety do not have the right to partition without the consent of both spouses.

A co-tenant with a future interest (e.g., remainder interest) does not have the right to partition since they do not have immediate possession of the property.

Partition in Kind: The court can physically divide the property into distinct portions, allowing each co-tenant to hold a separate portion.

Partition by Sale: If physical division is not feasible or fair, the court may order a sale of the property, with the proceeds divided among the co-tenants according to their ownership interests.

공동 연대 소유권자와 공동 지분 소유권자는 일방적으로 재산의 분할을 요청할 권리가 있다. 이 권리는 더 이상 재산을 공동으로 소유하기를 원하지 않을 때 재산을 나누거나 매각할 수 있도록 하는 것이다. 그러나 부부 공동 소유권자는 상대방 배우자의 동의 없이는 분할을 요청할 수 없다.

잔여권자(remainderman)와 같은 미래의 권리를 가진 공동 소유권자는 즉각적인 점유권이 없기 때문에 분할을 요청할 권리가 없다.

물리적 분할(Partition in Kind): 법원은 재산을 물리적으로 나누어 각 공동 소유권자가 독립적인 부분을 소유할 수 있도록 할 수 있다. 이는 실질적인 재산 분할이 가능한 경우에 사용된다.

매각에 의한 분할(Partition by Sale): 물리적으로 재산을 나누는 것이 불가능하거나 공정하지 않은 경우, 법원은 재산 매각을 명령할 수 있다. 매각된 재산의 수익은 공동 소유권자의 지분에 따라 나누어진다.

MEMO

Ⅱ | 임대인과 임차인(LANDLORD AND TENANT)

The relationship between a landlord and tenant creates a legal arrangement where the tenant is granted the right to use and possess real property for a specified time in exchange for rent. This relationship is primarily governed by a lease agreement, which outlines the rights and obligations of both the landlord and the tenant. The lease creates one of four possible leasehold estates, and these estates govern the nature of the tenant's interest in the property.

임대인과 임차인 간의 관계는 계약을 통해 형성되며, 임차인은 일정한 기간 동안 임대인의 부동산을 사용하고 점유할 권리를 얻는 대가로 임대료를 지불한다. 이 관계는 주로 임대차 계약에 의해 규율되며, 해 당 계약은 임대인과 임차인의 권리와 의무를 명시한다. 임대차 계약은 네 가지 가능한 임대차 중 하나가 성립되며, 이 임대차는 임차인이 부동산에 대해 가지는 권리의 성격을 결정한다.

A 임대차의 유형(Types of Tenancies)

1. 기간확정 임대차(Tenancy for Years)

A tenancy for years is a leasehold estate that lasts for a fixed period, which could be days, months, or years. It has a definite start and end date, and no notice is required to terminate the lease at the end of the term because the expiration is predetermined. The lease automatically terminates at the end of the agreed-upon term.

1) Term

A tenancy for years can be for any duration of time, such as one week, six months, or five years, as long as the period is fixed and ascertainable at the start of the lease. There is no minimum or maximum time limit, as long as the start and end dates are clearly defined.

2) Creation

A tenancy for years is created by an agreement between the landlord and the tenant. This agreement can be oral or written, but the Statute of Frauds applies if the lease is longer than one year, meaning it must be in writing to be enforceable.

3) Termination

A tenancy for years automatically terminates at the end of the lease term, without the need for notice by either party.

Example: A landlord leases an apartment to a tenant for one year. At the end of the year, the lease automatically terminates unless the parties agree to renew.

기간확정 임대차(tenancy for years)는 확정된 기간 동안의 임대차로, 그 기간은 며칠, 몇 달 또는 몇 년일 수 있다. 이 임대차는 명확한 시작일과 종료일이 있으며, 임대차 계약 기간이 종료하면 사전 통지 없이 자동으로 임대차는 종료된다.

1) 기간(Term)

기간확정 임대차는 1주, 6개월 또는 5년과 같은 확정된 기간 동안 유효하다. 시작일과 종료일이 임대차 계약의 시작 시점에서 명확하게 정해져 있으면 그 기간은 얼마든지 될 수 있으며, 최소 또는 최대 기간에 대한 제한은 없다.

2) 성립(Creation)

기간확정 임대차는 임대인과 임차인 간의 합의에 의해 성립되며, 이 합의는 구두 또는 서면으로 이루어질 수 있다. 그러나 임대 기간이 1년을 초과하는 경우에는 사기방지법(statute of frauds)이 적용되므로 서면으로 작성되어야 법적으로 집행이 가능해진다.

3) 종료(Termination)

예시: A landlord leases an apartment to a tenant for one year. 1년이 끝나면 별도의 합의가 없으면 임대차 계약은 자동으로 종료된다.

2. 기간반복 임대차(Periodic Tenancy)

A periodic tenancy is a leasehold estate that continues for a set period (e.g., month-to-month or year-to-year) until either the landlord or tenant gives notice to terminate. It automatically renews at the end of each period unless proper notice is given by either party.

1) Term

A periodic tenancy is an ongoing estate measured by fixed intervals (such as month-to-month or year-to-year) but without a fixed termination date. The lease continues indefinitely until one party gives notice to terminate.

The Statute of Frauds, which generally requires certain contracts to be in writing, does not apply to a periodic tenancy because it does not have a fixed term. Even oral agreements can create periodic tenancies.

2) Creation

a) Express Agreement

A periodic tenancy can be explicitly created when the landlord and tenant agree on a recurring lease period without specifying a termination date.

Example: The landlord conveys the property to the tenant "from year to year" or "month to month," creating a periodic tenancy.

b) By Implication

A periodic tenancy can be implied when (1) the lease agreement fails to mention a termination date but provides for rent payments at set intervals (e.g., rent is paid monthly but the lease doesn't state when it ends) or (2) an oral term of years lease is created, but it violates the Statute of Frauds.

Example: A landlord rents an apartment to a tenant, and the agreement provides for rent to be paid monthly, but no end date is specified. This creates a periodic tenancy by implication.

c) By Operation of Law

A periodic tenancy may arise by operation of law when a tenant remains in possession after the expiration of a lease for a term of years (a holdover tenant) and the landlord continues to accept rent, the relationship may convert into a periodic tenancy.

Example: A tenant's one-year lease expires, but the tenant remains in the apartment and continues paying rent, which the landlord accepts. This creates a periodic tenancy, on a month-to-month basis.

3) Termination

a) Notice Requirement

Because a periodic tenancy does not have a predetermined end date, it must be terminated by giving notice. The tenancy continues indefinitely until proper notice is given by one party.

b) Timing of Notice

Notice must be given before the beginning of the intended last period of the tenancy.

Example: In a month-to-month tenancy, if a tenant wants to move out by the end of July, they must provide notice before the start of July.

c) Length of Notice

The notice period required to terminate a periodic tenancy must generally be equal to the length of the tenancy period, unless otherwise agreed.

Example: For a month-to-month tenancy, at least one month's notice is required. For a week-to-week tenancy, one week's notice is required. For a year-to-year tenancy, six months' notice is traditionally required, though many states have shortened this to one month.

기간반복 임대차(periodic tenancy)는 일정한 기간(예: 월 단위, 연 단위) 동안 지속되며, 임대인 또는 임차인이 계약을 종료하기 위해 종료 통지를 할 때까지 자동으로 갱신되는 임대차다. 계약 기간이 끝날 때까지 통지하지 않으면 자동으로 다음 기간으로 갱신된다.

1) 기간(Term)

기간반복 임대차는 고정된 주기(예: 월 단위 또는 연 단위)로 측정되지만, 명확한 종료일이 없다. 임대차 계약은 당사자 중 일방이 통지를 하지 않는 한 무기한 지속된다.

사기방지법(statute of frauds)은 고정된 기간이 없는 기간반복 임대차에는 적용되지 않으며, 구두 합의만으로도 기간반복 임대차를 성립시킬 수 있다.

2) 성립(Creation)

a) 명시적 합의(Express Agreement)

기간반복 임대차는 임대인과 임차인이 반복적인 임대 기간에 대해 명시적으로 합의하고 종료일을 지정하지 않을 때 성립된다.

예시: The landlord conveys the property to the tenant "from year to year" or "month to month." 이러한 임대차는 기간반복 임대차가 성립하는 경우이다.

b) 묵시적 성립(By Implication)

기간반복 임대차는 다음과 같은 경우 묵시적으로 성립될 수 있다. 즉 (1) 임대차 계약서에 종료일이 명시되지 않았지만 일정한 간격으로 임대료 지급을 규정한 경우(예: 매월 임대료를 지불하지만 종료일이 명시되지 않은 경우) 또는 (2) 사기방지법을 위반한 구두로 계약된 기간확정 임대차가 있는 경우.

예시: 임대인이 임차인에게 아파트를 임대하며 매달 임대료를 지불하도록 계약했지만 종료일이 명시되지 않았다면, 이는 묵시적으로 기간반복 임대차가 성립되는 것이다.

c) 법률에 의한 성립(By Operation of Law)

기간반복 임대차는 법률에 의하여 성립할 수 있다. 예를 들어, 임차인이 기간확정 임대차 종료 후에도 부동산을 점유하고 있고 임대인이 임대료를 계속 수령할 경우, 그 관계는 기간반복 임대차로 전환될 수 있다.

예시: 임차인의 1년 임대차 계약이 종료되었지만, 임차인이 계속 아파트에 거주하고 임대인이 임대료를 수령하는 경우, 이는 월 단위의 기간반복 임대차로 전환된다.

3) 종료(Termination)

a) 통지 요건(Notice Requirement)

기간반복 임대차는 사전 통지에 의해 종료되어야 한다. 통지가 없으면 임대차 계약은 무기한 지속된다.

b) 통지 시기(Timing of Notice)

통지는 계약의 마지막 기간이 시작되기 전에 이루어져야 한다.

예시: 월 단위 임대에서, 임차인이 7월 말에 이사를 나가고 싶다면, 7월이 시작되기 전에 통지를 해야 한다.

c) 통지 기간(Length of Notice)

기간반복 임대차를 종료하기 위한 통지 기간은 일반적으로 임대 기간과 동일한 길이의 기간이어야 한다. 단, 합의된 경우는 예외이다.

예시: 월 단위 임대차의 경우 최소 1개월 전에 통지가 필요하다. 주 단위 임대차의 경우 1주일의 통지가 필요하다. 연 단위 임대차의 경우에는 전통적으로 6개월의 통지가 필요했지만, 많은 주에서는 이를 1개월로 단축했다.

3. 임의 임대차(Tenancy at Will)

A tenancy at will is a type of leasehold estate that has no fixed duration and may be terminated at any time by either the landlord or the tenant. This type of lease allows for flexibility and can be terminated by either party without a predetermined end date.

1) Term

A tenancy at will does not have a specific, fixed term. It continues until either the landlord or the tenant decides to terminate it. This arrangement provides flexibility, as it does not bind the parties to a set lease period and can continue indefinitely, as long as both parties agree.

2) Creation

Express Agreement: A tenancy at will can be created through an express agreement between the landlord and tenant.

Implied Creation: A tenancy at will can also arise by implication when a person is allowed to occupy the property without a formal lease agreement, often while the parties are negotiating a more permanent lease.

Conversion to Periodic Tenancy: If the tenant begins paying regular rent, the tenancy at will is typically converted into a periodic tenancy.

3) Termination

a) Common Law

At common law, either party could terminate the tenancy at will without notice, but the tenant had to be given a reasonable time to vacate the premises after termination.

b) Statutory Requirements

Advance Notice: Most states now require advance notice to terminate a tenancy at will. The amount of notice required is usually specified by statute, and in many cases, it mirrors the notice requirements for periodic tenancies (e.g., 30 days).

Termination by Tenant Only: In some states, only the tenant may terminate the tenancy at will, providing the tenant with more flexibility.

임의 임대차(tenancy at will)는 정해진 기간이 없는 임대차 형태로, 임대인 또는 임차인이 언제든지 임대차 계약을 종료할 수 있다. 이 유형의 임대차는 유연성을 제공하며, 양 당사자가 사전 종료일을 정하지 않은 상태에서 자유롭게 계약을 유지하거나 종료할 수 있다.

1) 기간(Term)

임의 임대차는 일정한 고정 기간이 없다. 임대인 또는 임차인이 계약을 종료하기로 결정할 때까지 지속되며, 양 당사자가 동의하는 한 무기한 지속될 수 있는 유연한 임대차 형태이다.

2) 성립(Creation)

a) 명시적 합의(Express Agreement)

임의 임대차는 임대인과 임차인 간의 명시적 합의를 통해 성립될 수 있다.

b) 묵시적 성립(Implied Creation)

임의 임대차는 형식적인 임대차 계약 없이 임차인이 부동산을 점유하는 경우에도 성립될 수 있다. 이러한 경우는 주로 더 영구적인 임대차 계약을 협상 중일 때 발생한다.

c) 기간반복 임대차로의 전환(Conversion to Periodic Tenancy)

임차인이 정기적으로 임대료를 지불하기 시작하면, 임의 임대차는 일반적으로 기간반복 임대차(periodic tenancy)로 전환된다.

3) 종료(Termination)

a) 보통법(Common Law)

보통법에 따르면, 어느 당사자든 사전 통지 없이 임의 임대차를 종료할 수 있지만, 임차인은 종료 후 일정 기간 내에 재산을 비울 수 있는 합리적인 시간이 주어져야 했다.

b) 제정법적 요구사항(Statutory Requirements)

사전 통지(Advance Notice): 대부분의 주에서는 이제 임의 임대차를 종료할 때 사전 통지를 요구한다. 필요한 통지 기간은 주 법률에 따라 규정되며, 많은 경우 기간반복 임대차의 통지 요구 사항(예: 30일 통지)과 유사하다.

임차인만의 종료 권한(Termination by Tenant Only): 일부 주에서는 임차인만이 임의 임대차를 종료할 수 있는 권리를 가지며, 임차인에게 더 많은 유연성을 제공한다.

4. 용인 임대차(Tenancy at Sufferance)

A tenancy at sufferance occurs when a tenant remains in possession of the property after the lease term has expired, without the landlord's consent. This situation creates a temporary status where the tenant is still bound by the terms of the expired lease, such as the obligation to pay rent, but is no longer lawfully entitled to stay on the premises.

1) Termination of a Tenancy at Sufferance

   a) Tenant's Departure: The tenancy at sufferance ends when the tenant voluntarily vacates the property.

   b) Eviction by the Landlord: The landlord can initiate eviction proceedings to remove the holdover tenant from the premises. Eviction is the legal remedy available to landlords to recover possession when the tenant overstays their lease.

   c) Landlord's Decision to Renew or Lease for Another Term: The landlord may choose to create a new tenancy by allowing the tenant to remain on the premises. If the landlord accepts rent for a new term, this may result in the creation of a periodic tenancy (e.g., month-to-month) or a lease for a new fixed term.

2) Landlord's Remedies

   In a tenancy at sufferance, the landlord has several options for addressing the holdover tenant:

   a) Eviction: The landlord may proceed with eviction to remove the tenant from the property.

   b) Periodic Tenancy: The landlord may choose to accept rent from the holdover tenant, which can lead to the creation of a periodic tenancy (e.g., month-to-month) based on the prior lease terms.

   c) Forcible Entry (in some states): In certain jurisdictions, the landlord may have the right to pursue forcible entry to reclaim the premises, though this is less common.

용인 임대차(tenancy at sufferance)는 임차인이 임대차 계약 기간이 만료된 후 임대인의 동의 없이 부동산을 계속 점유하는 경우 발생한다. 이 상황에서 임차인은 임대차 계약의 조건(예: 임대료 지급 등)을 계속 준수해야 하지만, 법적으로 부동산에 머무를 권리는 없다.

1) 용인 임대차의 종료(Termination of a Tenancy at Sufferance)

a) 임차인의 퇴거(Tenant's Departure): 임차인이 자발적으로 부동산을 비우면 용인 임대차는 종료된다.

b) 임대인의 퇴거 조치(Eviction by the Landlord): 임대인은 퇴거 절차를 시작하여 부동산에서 무단 점유 임차인을 퇴거시킬 수 있다. 퇴거는 임대인이 임차인의 계약 만료 후 부동산을 회복하기 위한 법적 구제책이다.

c) 임대인의 재계약 결정(Landlord's Decision to Renew or Lease for Another Term): 임대인은 임차인이 재산에 머무르는 것을 허용하여 새로운 임대차 계약을 체결할 수 있다. 만약 임대인이 새로운 기간에 대해 임대료를 수락하면, 기간반복 임대차(periodic tenancy) 또는 새롭게 확정된 기간의 임대차 계약이 성립될 수 있다.

2) 임대인의 구제책(Landlord's Remedies)

용인 임대차에서 임대인은 여러 가지 방법으로 무단 점유 임차인(holdover tenant)에 대응할 수 있다,

a) 퇴거(Eviction): 임대인은 임차인을 퇴거시키기 위한 법적 절차를 진행할 수 있다.

b) 기간반복 임대차(Periodic Tenancy): 임대인은 임차인의 임대료를 수락하여 기간반복 임대차를 성립시킬 수 있으며, 이는 기존 임대차 계약의 조건에 따라 결정된다.

c) 강제 진입(Forcible Entry): 일부 관할권에서는 임대인이 부동산을 회복하기 위해 강제 진입을 추구할 권리가 있을 수 있지만, 이는 드문 경우이다.

B 임차인의 의무(Duties of Tenant)

The relationship between a landlord and a tenant is governed by both the lease agreement and certain common law principles. The tenant has two primary duties: (1) to pay rent and (2) to avoid waste. Additionally, the tenant may have other contractual obligations under the lease. Below is a detailed explanation of these duties and the potential consequences for breach.

임대인과 임차인 간의 관계는 임대차 계약과 보통법 원칙에 의해 규율된다. 임차인은 두 가지 주요 의무를 가진다. 즉, 임대료 지급 의무와 부동산 훼손행위 금지 의무가 있다. 이 외에도 임차인은 임대차 계약에 명시된 계약상 의무를 가질 수 있다.

1. 임대료 지급 의무(Duty to Pay Rent)

The duty to pay rent is a fundamental obligation arising out of the lease agreement. Most leases require the tenant to pay rent at regular intervals (e.g., monthly), and this duty is enforceable regardless of other circumstances, with a few exceptions.

Apportionment: At common law, rent was not apportionable (i.e., tenants had to pay the entire rent regardless of when the lease ended). However, most modern jurisdictions now allow rent to be apportioned if the lease terminates early.

Security Deposit: In addition to rent, a landlord may require a security deposit to cover potential damage or unpaid rent.

Exceptions to the Duty to Pay Rent:

1) Destruction of the Premises

If the leased premises are destroyed (e.g., by fire or flood) and the tenant is not at fault, the lease is terminated, and the tenant is excused from paying rent. At common law, destruction of the premises did not excuse the tenant from paying rent, but modern statutes typically relieve the tenant from this duty.

b) Material Breach by the Landlord

If the landlord materially breaches the lease (e.g., failing to meet the implied warranty of habitability), the tenant may be relieved of the duty to pay rent.

임대료 지급 의무는 임대차 계약에서 발생하는 기본적인 의무로, 대부분의 임대차 계약은 임차인이 정기적인 간격(예: 매월)으로 임대료를 지불하도록 요구한다. 이 의무는 몇 가지 예외를 제외하고는 상황에 관계없이 법적으로 강제된다.

배분(Apportionment): 보통법상 임대료는 배분되지 않았으며, 임차인은 임대차 계약이 언제 종료되든지 상관없이 전체 임대료를 지불해야 했다. 그러나 현대 대부분의 관할권에서는 임대차 계약이 조기에 종료되는 경우 임대료를 배분할 수 있도록 허용하고 있다.

보증금(Security Deposit): 임대인은 임대료 외에도 부동산에 대한 잠재적인 훼손이나 미지급 임대료에 충당하기 위해 보증금을 요구할 수 있다.

임대료 지급 의무에 대한 예외(Exceptions to the Duty to Pay Rent)

1) 재산 파괴(Destruction of the Premises)

임차인이 잘못한 것이 아니고 임차한 부동산이 파괴된 경우(예: 화재 또는 홍수), 임대차 계약은 종료되며 임차인은 임대료 지급 의무에서 면제된다. 보통법에서는 재산 파괴가 임대료 지급을 면제하지 않았지만, 현대 법률에서는 대부분 임차인을 이 의무에서 면제하고 있다.

2) 임대인의 중대한 계약 위반(Material Breach by the Landlord)

임대인이 임대차 계약을 중대하게 위반하는 경우(예: 거주에 대한 묵시적 보증을 충족하지 못하는 경우), 임차인은 임대료 지급 의무에서 면제될 수 있다.

2. 훼손행위 금지 의무(Duty to Avoid Waste)

Tenants have a duty to avoid causing damage (waste) to the property. This duty is similar to the duty imposed on life tenants.

1) Affirmative Waste

The tenant must not intentionally damage or alter the property in a way that reduces its value (e.g., breaking fixtures or walls).

2) Permissive Waste

The tenant must take reasonable steps to prevent damage, such as maintaining the premises and performing minor repairs. However, tenants are not generally responsible for normal wear and tear unless specified in the lease.

3) Ameliorative Waste

The tenant must not make substantial changes to the property, even if those changes improve its value, without the landlord's consent. However, tenants may be entitled to make changes that are reasonably necessary for using the property, depending on the lease agreement.

임차인은 부동산에 대한 훼손(waste)을 방지할 의무가 있다. 이 의무는 종신소유권자에게 부과되는 의무와 유사하다.

1) 적극적 훼손행위(Affirmative Waste)

임차인은 부동산의 가치를 감소시키는 방식으로 고의적으로 훼손시키거나 변경해서는 안 된다(예: 설비나 벽을 파손하는 행위).

2) 소극적 훼손행위(Permissive Waste)

임차인은 부동산의 훼손을 방지하기 위해 합리적인 조치를 취해야 하며, 이는 부동산의 유지 관리 및 소규모 수리를 포함한다. 그러나 임대차 계약에 명시되지 않는 한, 일반적인 마모 및 손상(wear and tear)에 대해서는 임차인이 책임지지 않는다.

3) 개량적 훼손행위(Ameliorative Waste)

임차인은 임대인의 동의 없이 부동산의 가치를 높이는 변경을 포함하여, 부동산에 중대한 변경을 가해서는 안 된다. 그러나 임대차 계약에 따라 부동산 사용에 합리적으로 필요한 변경을 할 권리가 있을 수 있다.

3. 수리 의무(Duty to Repair)

1) Residential Leases

Provisions that impose a repair duty on the tenant are generally void, but tenants may be required to notify the landlord of needed repairs.

2) Non-Residential Leases

If the lease requires the tenant to "repair and maintain" the property, the tenant may be liable for all damage, unless caused by the landlord. However, many modern courts limit this duty to exclude major structural damage not caused by the tenant (e.g., damage due to a fire).

1) 주거용 임대차(Residential Leases)

임차인에게 수리 의무를 부과하는 조항은 일반적으로 무효이다. 그러나 임차인은 필요한 수리에 대해 임대인에게 통지해야 할 의무가 있을 수 있다.

2) 비주거용 임대차(Non-Residential Leases)

임대차 계약이 임차인에게 부동산을 "수리하고 유지할 것"을 요구하는 경우, 임차인은 임대인이 유발한 손해를 제외한 모든 손해에 대해 책임을 질 수 있다. 그러나 많은 현대 법원은 임차인이 유발하지 않은 주요 구조적 손해(예: 화재로 인한 손해)에 대해서는 이 의무를 제한하고 있다.

4. 기타 의무(Other Duties)

Compliance with Lease Terms: Tenants must adhere to all specific terms outlined in the lease, such as noise restrictions, pet policies, or business use limitations.

Illegal Activities: Using the property for illegal purposes (e.g., drug distribution) breaches the lease and can result in termination.

Good Faith Use: Tenants are expected to use the property in a manner consistent with the lease's purpose and in good faith.

임대차 조건 준수(Compliance with Lease Terms): 임차인은 임대차 계약서에 명시된 모든 특정 조건을 준수해야 한다. 이는 소음 제한, 반려동물 정책, 영업 목적 사용 제한 등의 조항을 포함한다.

불법 행위 금지(Illegal Activities): 부동산을 마약 유통과 같은 불법적인 목적으로 사용하는 것은 임대차 계약의 위반이며, 계약 종료의 결과를 초래할 수 있다.

신의성실의 원칙에 따른 사용(Good Faith Use): 임차인은 임대차의 목적과 신의성실의 원칙에 부합하는 방식으로 부동산을 사용해야 한다.

5. 임차인의 위반에 대한 임대인의 구제책 (Landlord's Remedies for Tenant's Breach)

1) Failure to Pay Rent

If the tenant fails to pay rent, the landlord can (1) sue for damages or (2) evict the tenant through legal proceedings. Late payment of rent is considered a material breach, allowing the landlord to take action.

2) Abandonment

If the tenant unjustifiably abandons the premises, the landlord may treat the abandonment as an offer to surrender and accept by retaking the property.

The landlord can re-rent the property on the tenant's behalf and hold the tenant liable for any deficiency (unpaid rent after re-renting the premises).

Duty to mitigate: The majority rule today requires the landlord to make reasonable efforts to mitigate damages by making an effort to re-rent the premises.

3) Holdover Tenant

A holdover tenant is one who remains in possession after the lease term has expired without the landlord's agreement.

The landlord can either (1) treat the tenant as a periodic tenant (e.g., month-to-month) by accepting rent or (2) treat the tenant as a tenant at sufferance and proceed with eviction.

4) Self-Help Eviction

In most states, landlords are no longer allowed to use self-help to evict a tenant (e.g., locking the tenant out or removing their belongings). Instead, the landlord must serve proper notice and obtain a court judgment of possession.

1) 임대료 미지급(Failure to Pay Rent)

임차인이 임대료를 지급하지 않는 경우, 임대인은 (1) 손해 배상을 청구하거나 (2) 법적 절차를 통해 임차인을 퇴거시킬 수 있다. 임대료의 지연 지급은 중대한 계약 위반으로 간주되어, 임대인이 법적 조치를 취할 수 있게 한다.

2) 점유포기(Abandonment)

임차인이 정당한 이유 없이 부동산의 점유를 포기한 경우, 임대인은 이를 임차인의 권리 포기 제안으로 간주하고, 재산을 재취득함으로써 이를 수락할 수 있다.

임대인은 임차인을 대신하여 부동산을 재임대하고, 발생한 부족분(재임대 후에도 남은 미지급 임대료)에 대해 임차인에게 책임을 물을 수 있다.

손해 경감 의무(Duty to Mitigate): 오늘날 다수의 법률에 따르면, 임대인은 재임대를 시도함으로써 손해를 합리적으로 경감하기 위한 노력을 해야 한다.

3) 무단 점유 임차인(Holdover Tenant)

무단 점유 임차인은 임대인의 동의 없이 임대 기간이 만료된 후에도 부동산을 계속 점유하는 임차인을 말한다.

임대인은 (1) 임대료를 수락하여 임차인을 기간반복 임차인(periodic tenant)으로 취급하거나 (2) 임차인을 임차인 용인 임차인(tenant at sufferance)으로 간주하여 퇴거 절차를 진행할 수 있다.

4) 자력 구제에 의한 퇴거(Self-Help Eviction)

대부분의 주에서는 임대인이 임차인을 퇴거시키기 위해 자력 구제(예: 임차인을 잠그거나 물건을 제거하는 행위)를 사용하는 것이 허용되지 않는다. 대신, 임대인은 적절한 통지를 제공하고 법원의 점유 판결을 받아야 한다.

C 임대인의 의무(Duties of Landlord)

Landlords have several important duties under residential and commercial leases that are designed to protect the tenant's rights to use, enjoy, and inhabit the property safely. Failure to fulfill these duties can result in legal consequences for the landlord and provide tenants with certain remedies.

임대인은 주거용 및 상업용 임대차에서 임차인의 안전한 부동산 사용, 향유 및 거주 권리를 보호하기 위해 여러 가지 중요한 의무를 가진다. 이러한 의무를 이행하지 못하면 임대인에게 법적 결과가 발생할 수 있으며, 임차인에게 일정한 구제책을 제공하게 된다.

1. 점유 제공 의무(Duty to Give Possession)

Actual Possession (Majority Rule): In most states, the landlord must deliver actual possession of the leased premises to the tenant at the start of the lease. If the landlord fails to do so, the tenant is relieved of the obligation to pay rent.

Legal Possession (Minority Rule): In some states, the landlord only needs to provide legal possession (the right to possess) without guaranteeing that the tenant can physically take possession.

실제 점유(Actual Possession, 다수의견): 대부분의 주에서는 임대인이 임대차 시작 시점에 임차인에게 임대 부동산의 실제 점유(actual possession)를 제공해야 한다. 임대인이 이를 이행하지 못하면, 임차인은 임대료 지급 의무에서 면제된다.

법적 점유(Legal Possession, 소수의견): 일부 주에서는 임대인이 임차인에게 부동산에 대한 법적 점유(legal possession), 즉 점유할 권리만 제공하면 되고, 임차인이 실제로 부동산을 점유할 수 있음을 보장할 필요는 없다.

2. 수리 의무(Duty to Repair)

Residential Leases: The landlord has the duty to keep the property in good repair in residential leases, even if the lease attempts to place the burden on the tenant. However, the landlord is not responsible for damage caused by the tenant.

Commercial Leases: The lease agreement can assign the duty to repair to the tenant in a commercial lease. Unless explicitly stated, landlords in commercial leases may not have the same repair obligations as in residential leases.

주거용 임대차(Residential Leases): 임차인에게 수리 의무를 부과하는 조항은 일반적으로 무효이다. 그러나 임차인은 필요한 수리에 대해 임대인에게 통지해야 할 의무가 있을 수 있다.

상업용 임대차(Commercial Leases): 상업용 임대차에서는 임대차 계약이 수리 의무를 임차인에게 할당할 수 있다. 명시적으로 규정되지 않는 한, 상업용 임대차에서 임대인은 주거용 임대차에서와 동일한 수리 의무를 가지지 않을 수 있다.

3. 거주적합성에 대한 묵시적 보증(Implied Warranty of Habitability)

Residential Leases: Most residential leases come with an implied warranty of habitability. This means the property must be maintained in a condition suitable for residential use, including compliance with housing codes and safety regulations.

Non-Waivable: The warranty cannot be waived by the tenant, even if they knowingly rent a property with defects.

Tenant's Remedies: If the property is not habitable, the tenant can (1) refuse to pay rent until the defect is remedied; (2) remedy the defect themselves and deduct the cost from their rent; or (3) defend against eviction if the landlord tries to remove them for non-payment of rent caused by habitability issues.

Before withholding rent or taking remedial action, the tenant must usually notify the landlord and provide a reasonable opportunity to fix the problem.

주거용 임대차(Residential Leases): 대부분의 주거용 임대차는 거주적합성에 대한 묵시적 보증이 있다. 이는 부동산이 주거용으로 적합한 상태로 유지되어야 하며, 주택법 및 안전 규정을 준수해야 함을 의미한다.

포기 불가(Non-Waivable): 거주적합성에 대한 묵시적 보증은 임차인이 하자가 있는 부동산을 알고 임차하더라도 포기가 되지 않는다.

임차인의 구제책(Tenant's Remedies): 부동산이 거주가 가능하지 않은 경우, 임차인은 다음과 같은 조치를 취할 수 있다. 즉, (1) 하자가 수정될 때까지 임대료 지급을 거부할 수 있다 (2) 스스로 하자를 수정하고 그 비용을 임대료에서 공제할 수 있다 또는 (3) 임대인이 거주적합성 문제로 인해 미지급된 임대료를 이유로 퇴거를 시도하는 경우, 이에 대한 항변사유가 될 수 있다.

임대료를 보류하거나 수리 조치를 취하기 전에, 임차인은 일반적으로 임대인에게 통지하고 하자를 해결할 수 있는 합리적인 기회를 제공해야 한다.

4. 평온한 권리 향유의 약정(Covenant of Quiet Enjoyment)

Both commercial and residential leases include an implied covenant of quiet enjoyment, which means the tenant has the right to peaceful possession without interference by the landlord, someone claiming through the landlord, or someone with superior title.

Breach by Landlord: If the landlord's actions, such as entering the property without notice or failing to fix severe maintenance issues, disrupt the tenant's possession, it could result in actual or constructive eviction.

Duty to Address Nuisances: While the landlord is not liable for the actions of other tenants, they must take action if a tenant's creates a nuisance or disrupts the quiet enjoyment of others, especially in common areas.

상업용과 주거용 임대차 모두에 평온한 권리 향유에 대한 묵시적 약정이 포함되어 있다. 이는 임차인이 임대인, 임대인을 통해 권리를 주장하는 자 또는 상위 권리자에 의한 간섭 없이 평온하게 부동산을 점유할 권리가 있음을 의미한다.

임대인의 위반(Breach by Landlord): 임대인이 사전 통지 없이 부동산에 출입하거나 심각한 유지 보수 문제를 해결하지 않는 등 임차인의 점유를 방해하는 행위를 하는 경우, 이는 실제 퇴거(actual eviction) 또는 의제적 퇴거(constructive eviction)의 결과를 초래할 수 있다.

생활방해 행위에 대한 조치 의무(Duty to Address Nuisances): 임대인은 다른 임차인의 행위에 대해 직접적인 책임을 지지 않지만, 특히 공용 공간에서 임차인의 행위가 생활방해(nuisance)를 일으키거나 다른 임차인의 평온한 권리 향유를 방해하는 경우에는 조치를 취해야 할 의무가 있다.

5. 퇴거와 관련된 구제책(Eviction and Related Remedies)

1) Actual Eviction

If the landlord physically removes the tenant from the property, this constitutes a total eviction, which terminates the lease and relieves the tenant of the obligation to pay rent.

2) Partial Eviction

If the tenant is prevented from using part of the property, different rules apply based on who is responsible for the eviction:

a) Landlord: If the landlord is responsible for the partial eviction, the tenant may stop paying rent for the entire premises, even if only a portion is affected.

b) Third Party with Superior Claim: If a third party with a superior legal claim (e.g., a rightful owner) evicts the tenant, the tenant must pay a reasonable rental value for the portion they still occupy.

c) Third-Party Trespasser: If a third party with no legal right evicts the tenant (e.g., a trespasser), the tenant must continue paying rent, and it is the landlord's responsibility to address the issue.

3) Constructive Eviction

If the landlord's failure to perform required duties (e.g., failing to provide heat, water, or repair severe issues) significantly interferes with the tenant's use of the property, this can amount to constructive eviction.

Tenant's Obligations: For a constructive eviction claim, the tenant must (1) notify the landlord of the problem and (2) vacate the property within a reasonable time if the landlord does not resolve the issue.

The tenant's obligation to pay rent is excused if constructive eviction is established.

4) Retaliatory Eviction

A landlord cannot evict a tenant in retaliation for reporting a housing code violation or exercising legal rights. Retaliatory eviction is illegal, and the tenant may have a defense to eviction or other remedies available.

1) 실제 퇴거(Actual Eviction)

임대인이 임차인을 부동산에서 물리적으로 나가게 하는 경우, 이는 완전한 퇴거로 간주되며, 임대차 계약을 종료시키고 임차인의 임대료 지급 의무를 면제하게 한다.

2) 부분 퇴거(Partial Eviction)

임차인이 부동산의 일부를 사용하는 것이 방해받는 경우, 누가 퇴거에 책임이 있는지에 따라 다른 원칙이 적용된다.

a) 임대인(Landlord): 임대인이 부분 퇴거에 책임이 있는 경우, 임차인은 비록 부동산의 일부에 영향을 받는 경우라 하더라도 전체 부동산에 대한 임

대료 지급을 중단할 수 있다.

b) 우월한 권리를 가진 제3자(Third Party with Superior Claim): 우월한 법적 권리(예: 정당한 소유자)를 가진 제3자가 임차인을 퇴거시키는 경우, 임차인은 여전히 점유하고 있는 부분에 대한 합리적인 임대료를 지불해야 한다.

c) 무단 침입한 제3자(Third-Party Trespasser): 법적 권리가 없는 제3자(예: 무단 침입자)가 임차인을 퇴거시키는 경우, 임차인은 임대료를 계속 지불해야 하며, 이 문제를 해결할 책임은 임대인에게 있다.

3) 의제적 퇴거(Constructive Eviction)

임대인이 필요한 의무를 이행하지 못하여(예: 난방, 물 제공 실패 또는 심각한 하자에 대한 수리 불이행), 임차인의 부동산 사용을 상당히 방해하는 경우, 이는 의제적 퇴거에 해당할 수 있다.

임차인의 의무(Tenant's Obligations): 의제적 퇴거 클레임을 위해, 임차인은 (1) 하자에 대해 임대인에게 통지해야 하고 (2) 임대인이 하자를 해결하지 않을 경우 합리적인 기간 내에 부동산을 비워야 한다.

의제적 퇴거가 성립되면 임차인의 임대료 지급 의무는 면제된다.

4) 보복적 퇴거(Retaliatory Eviction)

임대인은 주택규정 위반 사항을 신고하거나 법적 권리를 행사한 것에 대한 보복으로 임차인을 퇴거시킬 수 없다. 보복적 퇴거는 불법이며, 임차인은 퇴거에 대한 항변 또는 다른 구제책을 가질 수 있다.

D 불법행위 책임(Tort Liabilities)

Both landlords and tenants may have tort liability for injuries occurring on the leased property. Their responsibilities and potential liabilities depend on their control over the property and the specific circumstances under which the injury occurs.[4]

임대인과 임차인 모두 임대 부동산에서 발생하는 상해에 대해 불법행위 책임을 질 수 있다. 불법행위에 대한 책임과 잠재적 법적 책임은 부동산에 대한 통제력과 상해가 발생한 구체적인 상황에 따라 달라진다.

1. 임차인의 불법행위 책임(Tenant's Tort Liability)

The tenant, as the possessor of the leasehold, owes a duty of care to people who enter the property, including invitees, licensees, or and foreseeable trespassers and can be liable for dangerous conditions or activities on the leased property.

임차인은 임대 부동산의 점유자로서, 부동산에 들어오는 사람들, 즉 초대된 자(invitees), 허가된 자(licensees) 및 예측 가능한 무단침입자(foreseeable trespassers)에 대하여 주의의무(duty of care)를 부담한다. 따라서 임차인은 임차 부동산에서 발생하는 위험한 상태나 활동으로 인한 상해에 대해 책임을 질 수 있다.

4) 불법행위 책임에 대한 자세한 내용은 The Law of Torts (미국 불법행위법, 2024.3, 강병진 저) 도서에 설명되어 있음.

2. 임대인의 불법행위 책임(Landlord's Tort Liability)

At common law, landlords had limited liability for injuries occurring on leased property, but modern legal trends have expanded their responsibilities.

1) Under Common Law

The landlord is liable for injuries occurring in common areas (e.g., hallways, stairways, parking lots) that the landlord maintains and controls.

The landlord is also responsible for injuries in areas under their control, even if not common to all tenants.

The landlord can be liable for injuries caused by hidden defects that the tenant was not aware of at the time of leasing but the landlord knew about or should have known about.

If the landlord undertakes repairs but does so negligently, resulting in injuries, they may be liable.

2) Modern Trend

The modern legal trend holds landlords to a general duty of reasonable care regarding the safety of tenants and visitors.

Landlords may be liable for injuries caused by defects that existed before the tenant took possession of the property, especially if the landlord failed to disclose or repair the defect.

Landlords are responsible for maintaining the property according to applicable housing codes. Failure to make necessary repairs or address dangerous conditions that violate the housing code can result in liability if someone is injured.

In some cases, landlords may be held liable for injuries caused by criminal activities of third parties if the landlord failed to take reasonable precautions in light of known risks (e.g., failure to provide adequate security in a high-crime area).

보통법상, 임대인은 임대 부동산에서 발생한 상해에 대해 제한된 책임만을 졌지만, 현대의 법적 경향은 임대인의 책임을 확대하고 있다.

1) 보통법(Under Common Law)

임대인은 임대인이 관리 및 통제하는 공용 구역(예: 복도, 계단, 주차장)에서 발생한 상해에 대해 책임을 진다.

임대인의 통제 하에 있는 구역에서 발생한 상해에 대해서도, 그 구역이 모든 임차인에게 공용이 아니더라도 임대인은 책임을 진다.

임대인은 임차인이 임대 시점에 알지 못했지만, 임대인이 알고 있었거나 알았어야 할 숨겨진 하자로 인한 상해에 대해 책임을 질 수 있다.

임대인이 수리를 시도했으나 부주의하게 수행하여 상해가 발생한 경우, 임대인은 책임을 질 수 있다.

2) 현대적 경향(Modern Trend)

현대의 법적 경향은 임대인에게 임차인과 방문자의 안전에 대해 일반적인 합리적 주의 의무를 부담시키고 있다.

임대인은 임차인이 부동산을 점유하기 전에 존재했던 하자로 인한 상해에 대해 책임을 질 수 있으며, 특히 임대인이 그 하자를 공개하거나 수리하지 않은 경우 그렇다.

임대인은 적용 가능한 주택 규정에 따라 부동산을 유지할 책임이 있다. 필요한 수리를 하지 않거나 주택 규정을 위반하는 위험한 상태를 해결하지 않아 상해가 발생한 경우, 임대인은 책임을 질 수 있다.

일부 경우에는 임대인이 알려진 위험에 비추어 합리적인 예방 조치를 취하지 않은 경우(예: 범죄율이 높은 지역에서 적절한 보안을 제공하지 않은 경우), 제3자의 범죄 행위로 인한 상해에 대해 임대인이 책임을 질 수 있다.

E 양도 및 전대차(Assignment and Subletting)

A tenant has the right to assign or sublet a lease unless there is language in the lease that explicitly prohibits it. An assignment transfers the entire lease term to a new tenant, while a sublease transfers less than the entire lease term, with the original tenant retaining some interest. Both assignment and subletting create distinct legal relationships and liabilities.

임차인은 임대차 계약에서 명시적으로 이를 금지하는 조항이 없는 한, 임대차를 양도하거나 전대할 권리가 있다. 양도와 전대는 서로 구별되며, 각 경우에 관련된 당사자들에게 서로 다른 권리와 책임을 발생시킨다.

1. 양수인의 권리 및 책임(Assignee's Rights and Liabilities)

Privity of Estate with the Landlord: An assignee (the person who takes over the entire lease) enters into privity[5] of estate with the landlord. This means that the assignee is directly liable to the landlord for paying rent and for complying with all lease covenants that "run with the land" (i.e., relate to the use and enjoyment of the property).

Termination of Liability Upon Reassignment: If the assignee subsequently reassigns the leasehold to another tenant, the privity of estate between the assignee and the landlord ends. The new assignee assumes liability, and the previous assignee is no longer liable to the landlord.

임대인과의 부동산 관계(Privity of Estate with the Landlord): 양수인(임대차

5) Privity는 법적인 관계를 의미한다. 부동산법에서 privity of contract는 계약 당사자들 사이에 존재하는 법적 관계를 의미하며, privity of estate는 부동산의 권리와 의무의 연속성을 의미한다.

전체를 인수한 자)은 임대인과 부동산 관계(privity of estate)를 맺고 있다. 이는 양수인이 임대인에게 임대료를 지급하고, 부동산에 귀속하는 약정, 즉 부동산의 사용 및 향유와 관련된 모든 임대차의 약정을 준수할 직접적인 책임이 있음을 의미한다.

재양도 시 책임의 종료(Termination of Liability Upon Reassignment): 양수인이 이후에 임대차를 다른 임차인에게 재양도하는 경우, 양수인과 임대인 간의 부동산 관계는 종료된다. 새로운 양수인이 책임을 인수하며, 이전 양수인은 더 이상 임대인에게 책임을 지지 않는다.

2. 전차인의 권리 및 책임(Sublessee's Rights and Liabilities)

No Privity with the Landlord: A sublessee (the person who subleases part of the lease term from the original tenant) is not in privity of estate or privity of contract with the landlord. Therefore, the sublessee is not liable to the landlord for rent or any covenants under the original lease.

Liability to the Original Tenant (Lessee): The sublessee's obligations run to the original tenant, not the landlord. The sublessee is liable to the original tenant for rent and other terms under the sublease agreement.

Express Assumption of Liability: If the sublessee expressly assumes the rent or any other covenants in the lease, they become personally liable to the landlord for those obligations.

Enforcement of Covenants: The sublessee can enforce covenants made by the original tenant in the sublease agreement, but they cannot enforce any covenants made by the landlord in the original lease.

임대인과의 관계 부존재(No Privity with the Landlord): 전차인(원 임차인으로부터 임대 기간의 일부를 전대 받는 사람)은 임대인과 부동산 관계(privity of estate)나 계약 관계(privity of contract)가 없다. 따라서 전차인은 임대인에게 임대료나 원 임대차의 약정에 대해 책임을 지지 않는다.

원 임차인에 대한 책임(Liability to the Original Tenant): 전차인의 의무는 임대인이 아닌 원 임차인에게 귀속된다. 전차인은 전대 계약서에 따라 임대료 및 기타 조건에 대해 원 임차인에게 책임이 있다.

책임의 명시적 인수(Express Assumption of Liability): 전차인이 임대료나 임대차의 다른 약정을 명시적으로 인수하는 경우, 전차인은 해당 의무에 대해 임대인에게 개인적으로 책임을 진다.

약정의 이행(Enforcement of Covenants): 전차인은 전대 계약서에서 원 임차인이 한 약정을 이행하게 할 수 있지만, 원 임대차에서 임대인이 한 약정은 이행하게 할 수 없다.

3. 원 임차인의 권리 및 책임(Original Tenant's Rights and Liabilities)

Privity of Contract with the Landlord: Even after a successful assignment, the original tenant (lessee) remains in privity of contract with the landlord, meaning they are secondarily liable for rent and all other covenants in the lease.

Secondary Liability: If the assignee fails to meet their obligations (e.g., non-payment of rent), the original tenant remains liable to the landlord unless the landlord agrees to release the original tenant from liability (a novation).

Privity of Estate Terminates: The original tenant's privity of estate ends after an assignment, but they remain bound by the lease through privity of contract unless released by the landlord.

임대인과의 계약 관계(Privity of Contract with the Landlord): 성공적인 양도 후에도, 원 임차인(lessee)은 임대인과 계약 관계를 유지하므로, 임대료 및 임대차의 모든 약정에 대해 2차적으로 책임을 진다.

2차적 책임(Secondary Liability): 양수인이 자신의 의무(예: 임대료 미지급)를 이행하지 못하면, 임대인이 원 임차인을 책임에서 면제하기로 동의하지 않는 한, 원 임차인은 임대인에게 계속해서 책임을 진다.

부동산 관계의 종료(Privity of Estate Terminates): 양도 후 원 임차인의 부동산 관계는 종료되지만, 임대인이 면제하지 않는 한 계약 관계를 통해 임대차에 구속된다.

4. 임대인의 양도(Landlord Assignments)

Right to Assign: A landlord can generally assign their rights under the lease to a third party without tenant's consent unless the lease specifies otherwise. The tenant is required to pay rent to the new landlord (assignee) and comply with any lease covenants that run with the land.

Landlord's Continued Liability: Despite the assignment, the original landlord (assignor) remains liable to the tenant for all covenants in the lease, even after the assignment.

Assignee Landlord's Obligations: The new landlord (assignee) is bound by the terms of the lease and must fulfill the covenants that "run with the land" (e.g., maintaining common areas or providing services as stipulated in the lease).

양도 권리(Right to Assign): 임대인은 임대차에서 달리 규정하지 않는 한, 일반적으로 임차인의 동의 없이 임대차상의 권리를 제3자에게 양도할 수 있다. 임차인은 새로운 임대인(양수인)에게 임대료를 지급하고, 부동산에 귀속하는 임대차 약정을 준수해야 한다.

임대인의 지속적 책임(Landlord's Continued Liability): 양도에도 불구하고, 원 임대인(양도인)은 임대차의 모든 약정에 대해 임차인에게 계속해서 책임을 진다.

양수인 임대인의 의무(Assignee Landlord's Obligations): 새로운 임대인(양수인)은 임대차 조건에 구속되며, 부동산에 귀속하는 약정(예: 공용 구역의 유지, 임대차에 명시된 서비스 제공)을 이행해야 한다.

III | 점유취득시효(ADVERSE POSSESSION)

Under the doctrine of adverse possession, a trespasser can gain legal ownership of real property if they occupy the land for a specific period and meet certain legal requirements. Over time, the trespasser's possession can "ripen" into legal title, meaning that the trespasser becomes the lawful owner of the property. However, government-owned land is exempt from adverse possession and cannot be acquired this way.

점유취득시효의 원칙에 따르면, 무단 점유자는 특정 기간 동안 토지를 점유하고 일정한 법적 요건을 충족하면 부동산의 법적 소유권을 취득할 수 있다. 시간이 지남에 따라, 무단 점유자의 점유는 법적 소유권으로 성숙하여, 무단 점유자가 해당 재산의 합법적인 소유자가 되는 것이다. 그러나 정부 소유의 토지는 취득시효의 대상에서 제외되며 이러한 방식으로 획득될 수 없다.

A 점유취득시효의 요건(Requirements for Adverse Possession)

1. 계속적 점유(Continuous Possession)

The possession must be uninterrupted and last for the statutory period, which varies by jurisdiction (e.g., 10, 15, or 20 years). Seasonal use may qualify if it aligns with the typical use of the property, such as a summer camp.

Example: Sam uses a cabin on a remote piece of land for summer vacations every year for 15 years, consistent with how a vacation cabin is typically used. Even though Sam only uses the property seasonally, this may still count as continuous possession since it aligns with the type of property being used (a summer cabin).

1) Tacking

The current possessor may tack (add) their time of possession to that of a previous adverse possessor to meet the statutory period, provided they are in privity (a non-hostile relationship, such as through inheritance, deed, or contract). The possession must pass directly without gaps.

Example: John lives on a piece of land for 5 years, and then sells his interest (through a contract) to Kate, who continues living on the land for another 7 years. Since John and Kate are in privity (a contractual relationship), Kate can "tack" John's 5 years to her own 7 years, meeting the statutory requirement of 12 years for adverse possession.

No Tacking in Case of Ouster: If one adverse possessor wrongfully excludes another from the property, tacking is not allowed.

2) Disability of Owner

The statute of limitations for adverse possession does not run against a true owner who is under a legal disability (e.g., insanity, infancy, imprisonment) at the time the adverse possession began.

Example: If the true owner of the land is 10 years old when James begins occupying the property, the statute of limitations for adverse possession will not start until the owner turns 18 (reaches the age of majority). Only then does James's adverse possession time begin.

점유는 방해받지 않고 법정 기간 동안 지속되어야 하며, 이 법정 기간은 관할권에 따라 다르다(예: 10년, 15년 또는 20년). 일정 기간의 사용도 재산의 일반적인 사용 방식에 부합한다면 인정될 수 있다(예: 여름철 캠프장).

예시: 샘은 15년 동안 매년 여름 휴가로 외딴 토지에 있는 오두막을 사용한다. 이는 휴가용 오두막의 일반적인 사용 방식에 부합한다. 샘이 부동산을 여름 유가로

만 사용하더라도, 이는 해당 재산 유형(여름용 오두막)의 사용 방식과 일치하기 때문에 계속적인 점유로 인정될 수 있다.

1) 기간 합산(Tacking)

현재의 점유자는 이전의 점유자의 점유 기간을 자신의 기간에 합산하여 법정 기간을 충족할 수 있다. 단, 현재의 점유자와 이전의 점유자는 법적 관계(privity)(상속, 증서 또는 계약과 같은 비적대적인 관계)를 가지고 있어야 한다. 점유는 중단 없이 직접적으로 이어져야 한다.

예시: 존은 어떤 토지에서 5년 동안 살다가, 자신의 부동산 권리를 케이트에게 계약을 통해 매도한다. 케이트는 그 토지에서 추가로 7년 동안 계속 산다. 존과 케이트는 계약 관계가 있으므로, 케이트는 존의 5년을 자신의 7년에 합산하여 점유취득시효의 12년 법정 기간을 충족할 수 있다.

배제의 경우 연결 불가(No Tacking in Case of Ouster): 취득시효 점유자가 다른 점유자를 부당하게 부동산에서 배제한 경우, 배제된 점유자의 기간을 합산하는 것은 허용되지 않는다.

2) 소유자의 무능력(Disability of Owner)

취득시효의 법정 시효는 취득시효가 시작될 때 법적 무능력 상태(예: 정신질환, 미성년, 수감 중)에 있는 진정한 소유자에게는 적용되지 않는다.

예시: 토지의 진정한 소유자가 10살일 때, 제임스가 그 부동산을 점유하기 시작했다면, 취득시효는 소유자가 18세(성년 나이)에 도달할 때까지 시작되지 않는다. 소유자가 성년이 된 이후에야 비로소 제임스의 취득시효 기간이 시작된다.

2. 현실적이고 공개적이며 명백한 점유(Actual, Open, and Notorious)

The possession must be visible and apparent to a reasonable observer, such that the true owner could become aware of the adverse claim. Hidden uses, such as underground wiring, do not meet this requirement.

Example: Maria builds a fence around a plot of land, plants a garden, and regularly uses the space as her backyard. The true owner would easily be able to see Maria's use of the land. This satisfies the open and notorious requirement.

Example: If A lays underground cables on a piece of land, but otherwise does not use the land in any noticeable way, this would not meet the "open and notorious" requirement because the true owner may have no reason to know the land is being used.

점유는 합리적인 관찰자에게 명백하고 분명해야 하며, 진정한 소유자가 취득시효 주장을 알 수 있어야 한다. 지하에 전선을 설치하는 것과 같이 숨겨진 사용은 이 요건을 충족하지 않는다.

예시: 마리아는 토지에 울타리를 세우고, 정원을 가꾸며, 그 공간을 자신의 뒷마당처럼 정기적으로 사용한다. 진정한 소유자는 마리아의 재산 사용을 쉽게 알 수 있다. 이는 공개적이고 명백한 요건을 충족한다.

예시: A가 어떤 토지에 지하 케이블을 설치하지만, 그 외에는 눈에 띄는 방식으로 토지를 사용하지 않는다면, 이는 공개적이고 명백한 요건을 충족하지 못한다. 진정한 소유자는 그 토지가 사용되고 있다는 것을 알 이유가 없기 때문이다.

3. 적대적 점유(Hostile Possession)

The possession must be without the true owner's permission and with an intent to claim the land. "Hostile" in this context doesn't necessarily mean aggressive - it simply means the possessor is using the property without the owner's consent and with an intent to claim it as their own.

Example: Emma mistakenly believes a piece of land belongs to her (she was given incorrect boundary information). She builds a shed on the land and uses it as if it were hers. This is hostile because Emma is acting without permission, even though she mistakenly believes she owns the land.

점유는 진정한 소유자의 허가 없이 이루어져야 하며, 해당 토지를 자신의 것으로 주장하려는 의도를 가져야 한다. 여기서 "적대적"이라는 것은 반드시 공격적이라는 의미가 아니라, 단순히 소유자의 동의 없이 그 재산을 자신의 것으로 사용하고 있다는 것을 의미한다.

예시: 엠마는 잘못된 토지 경계 정보를 받아서 어떤 토지가 자신의 것이라고 잘못 믿었다. 그녀는 그 토지에 창고를 짓고, 자신의 것처럼 사용하였다. 이는 엠마가 소유자의 허가 없이 점유를 하고 있으므로 비록 그녀가 그 토지가 자신의 것이라고 잘못 믿고 있더라도적대적 점유에 해당한다.

4. 배타적 점유(Exclusive Possession)

The possession must be exclusive, meaning the adverse possessor cannot share possession with the true owner. However, multiple adverse possessors can jointly claim possession to create a tenancy in common.

Example: If A occupies a plot of land and builds a house on it, A cannot allow the original owner to use the land or share the house. He must act as though he is the sole owner of the property.

Example: If two friends, A and B, both build houses on the same plot of land and use it as their private property, they may be able to claim the land as co-owners through adverse possession.

점유는 배타적이어야 하며, 이는 취득시효 점유자가 진정한 소유자와 점유를 공유할 수 없음을 의미한다. 그러나 다수의 취득시효 점유자들이 함께 점유하여 공동 지분 소유권을 형성할 수 있다.

예시: A가 어떤 토지를 점유하고 그 위에 집을 지었다면, A는 원래 소유자에게 그 토지를 사용하거나 집을 공유하도록 허용해서는 안 된다. 그는 자신이 그 재산의 유일한 소유자인 것처럼 점유를 해야 한다.

예시: 두 친구 A와 B가 같은 토지에 각각 집을 짓고, 자신의 사유 재산처럼 사용한다면, 그들은 점유취득시효를 통해 공동 소유권자로서 그 토지의 소유권을 주장할 수 있다.

B 점유의 범위(Scope of Possession)

1) Constructive Adverse Possession

If the possessor occupies only part of the land but holds a color of title (i.e., a facially valid deed or will) to the entire property, they may gain title to the entire tract of land, provided they possess a reasonable portion of it.

Example: Alice occupies and farms a portion of a 100-acre plot described in a faulty deed she received. Even though she physically possesses only 20 acres, she could acquire all 100 acres through constructive adverse possession if her possession was continuous, hostile, and met the statutory requirements.

2) Subsurface Rights

The adverse possessor typically gains rights to the subsurface, such as minerals, unless these rights are owned by a third party.

3) Future Interests

The adverse possessor gains the interest of the person who held legal possession when the adverse possession began. The adverse possession does not run against future interests that exist at the time the adverse possession begins, but it does apply to future interests created later from a fee simple absolute estate.

Example: Mike starts adverse possession of land owned by a life tenant (Sarah) under a life estate. Mike's possession will affect Sarah's life estate, but not the remainder interest held by Paul (the future interest holder). Paul's clock for adverse possession starts only when Sarah's life estate ends, and Paul's future interest becomes possessory.

1) 의제적 점유취득시효 (Constructive Adverse Possession)

점유자가 재산의 일부만 점유하지만, 전체 부동산에 대하여 외관상 유효한 권원(color of title), 즉 외견상 유효한 증서나 유언서를 보유하고 있는 경우, 합리적인 부분을 점유하고 있다면 전체 토지에 대한 소유권을 취득할 수 있다.

예시: 앨리스는 하자가 있는 증서를 받아서 명시된 100에이커의 토지 중 일부를 점유하고 농사를 짓는다. 비록 그녀가 물리적으로 20에이커만 점유하고 있더라도, 그녀의 점유가 계속적이고 적대적이며 점유취득시효의 법정 요건을 충족한다면, 의제적 취득시효를 통해 전체 100에이커에 대한 소유권을 취득할 수 있다.

2) 지하권 (Subsurface Rights)

점유취득시효 점유자는 일반적으로 광물과 같은 지하권을 취득하게 되며, 단 이 권리가 제3자에 의해 소유되고 있지 않은 경우에 한한다.

3) 미래의 권리 (Future Interests)

점유취득시효 점유자는 취득시효가 시작될 때 법적 소유를 가진 사람의 권리를 취득한다. 취득시효는 취득시효가 시작될 때 존재하는 미래의 권리에 대해서는 적용되지 않지만, 절대적 단순 소유권(fee simple absolute estate)에서 이후에 성립된 미래의 권리에는 적용된다.

예시: 마이크가 종신소유권(life estate)을 가진 사라가 소유한 토지를 취득시효로 점유하기 시작한다. 마이크의 점유는 사라의 종신소유권에 영향을 미치지만, 미래의 권리를 가진 폴(잔여권자)의 권리에는 영향을 미치지 않는다. 폴의 취득시효 기간은 사라의 종신소유권이 종료하고 폴의 미래의 권리가 점유할 수 있는 소유권으로 전환될 때부터 시작된다.

IV | 토지 양도(LAND CONVEYANCE)

Land conveyance refers to the legal process of transferring ownership of real property from one party (the grantor) to another (the grantee).

토지의 양도는 한 당사자(양도인)로부터 다른 당사자(양수인)에게 부동산의 소유권을 이전하는 법적 절차를 의미한다.

A 토지매매계약(Land Sale Contract)

A land conveyance usually begins with a contract of sale between the buyer (grantee) and seller (grantor). The contract outlines essential terms like the purchase price and property description.

A contract for the sale of real property is generally governed by the same principles as any other contract, requiring offer, acceptance, and consideration. However, the contract must also comply with the Statute of Frauds.

토지의 양도는 일반적으로 매수인(양수인)과 매도인(양도인) 간의 매매계약으로 시작된다. 이 계약은 매수 가격과 토지에 대한 설명을 포함한 필수적인 조건들을 명시하고 있다.

토지 매매계약은 일반적으로 다른 계약과 동일한 원칙에 따라 규율되며, 이는 청약(offer), 승낙(acceptance) 및 약인(consideration)을 필요로 한다. 그러나 토지 매매계약은 사기방지법(statute of frauds)을 준수해야 한다.

1. 사기방지법(Statute of Frauds)

1) Writing Requirement

The contract must be in writing to satisfy the Statute of Frauds, which is essential in contracts for the sale of land. Oral agreements for the sale of real estate are generally unenforceable. The contract must be signed by the party to be charged (the party against whom enforcement is sought).

2) Essential Terms

The land sale contract must include essential terms: The contract must clearly identify the buyer and the seller. The contract must include a reasonably definite description of the property being sold. The contract must specify the price of the property and the terms of payment.

1) 서면 요구(Writing Requirement)

토지 매매계약은 사기방지법을 만족시키기 위해 서면으로 작성되어야 한다. 토지 매매에 대한 구두 합의는 일반적으로 이행을 강제할 수 없다. 계약의 이행을 청구 받는 자의 서명이 있어야 한다.

2) 필수 조건(Essential Terms)

토지 매매계약은 필수 조건들을 포함해야 한다. 즉, 계약은 매도인과 매수인이 명확해야 하고, 매도되는 토지에 대한 합리적으로 명확한 설명을 포함해야 하며, 토지의 가격과 지급 조건을 명시해야 한다.

2. 사기방지법의 예외(Exceptions to the Statute of Frauds)

While a written agreement is generally required, there are exceptions where an oral agreement may still be enforceable.

1) Part Performance

Under the doctrine of part performance, a party can seek specific performance of an oral land sale contract if certain acts of performance strongly suggest that a contract exists. Typically, courts require at least two of the following: (1) Payment of all or part of the purchase price; (2) Possession by the purchaser; or (3) Substantial improvement to the property.

2) Detrimental Reliance

Under the doctrine of detrimental reliance, specific performance of an oral contract may be available if the party seeking enforcement has reasonably relied on the agreement and would suffer significant hardship if the contract were not enforced. The other party may be estopped from using the Statute of Frauds as a defense.

Example: If a buyer incurs significant expenses (e.g., selling their current home or moving) based on an oral agreement, the court may enforce the contract to prevent undue hardship.

3) Admission

If the party against whom the contract is being enforced admits the existence of the contract in court or in writing, the Statute of Frauds may not be used as a defense.

토지 매매계약은 사기방지법에 따라 서면 계약이 일반적으로 요구되지만, 구두 계약이어도 이행을 강제할 수 있는 예외가 있다.

1) 부분 이행(Part Performance)

일부 이행의 원칙에 따라, 어떤 행위가 계약의 존재를 강력하게 시사하는 경우, 당사자는 구두에 의한 토지 매매계약의 이행을 청구할 수 있다. 일반적으로 법원은 다음 중 최소 두 가지를 요구한다. 즉, (1) 매수 가격의 전부 또는 일부 지불 (2) 매수인의 점유 또는 (3) 토지에 대한 상당한 개발 중 두 가지의 행위가 있는 경우 일부 이행의 원칙이 적용될 수 있다.

2) 손해유발 신뢰(Detrimental Reliance)

손해유발 신뢰의 원칙에 따라, 계약의 이행을 원하는 당사자가 계약에 합리적으로 의존하였고, 계약이 집행되지 않으면 상당한 어려움을 겪을 경우, 구두 계약의 특정 이행이 가능할 수 있다. 이 경우 상대방은 사기방지법을 항변사유로 사용하는 것이 금지될 수 있다.

예시: 매수인이 구두 합의에 기반하여 상당한 비용(예: 현재 집을 매도하거나 이사)을 발생시킨 경우, 법원은 부당한 어려움을 방지하기 위해 계약의 이행을 강제할 수 있다.

3) 인정(Admission)

계약의 이행을 요구받는 당사자가 법정이나 서면에서 계약의 존재를 인정하는 경우, 사기방지법은 항변사유로 사용될 수 없다.

3. 토지 매매계약에서의 상품성 있는 소유권 (Marketable Title in Land Sale Contracts)

In the sale of real property, there is typically an implied covenant of marketable title unless the contract states otherwise.

1) Marketable title

Marketable title refers to a title that is free from an unreasonable risk of litigation. A seller is generally required to provide marketable title at closing, meaning that the title must be free from encumbrances or defects that would expose the buyer to future legal disputes.

2) Merger Doctrine

Once the deed is delivered, the terms of the contract merge with the deed. After this merger, the buyer can no longer enforce the provisions of the land sale contract unless those terms are specifically included in the deed.

3) Defects That Make Title Unmarketable

Several conditions can render title unmarketable, including:

a) Private Encumbrances: A title encumbered by private restrictions such as mortgages, covenants, options, or easements is unmarketable unless the buyer explicitly agrees to accept the property subject to these encumbrances.

b) Zoning Violations: If the property is in violation of a zoning ordinance, the title may be deemed unmarketable. However, merely being subject to zoning laws does not affect marketability/-.

c) Title Acquired by Adverse Possession (Not Quieted): If the seller's title was obtained through adverse possession but has not been formally confirmed through a quiet title action (i.e., judicial decree), the title is considered unmarketable because of the risk of challenge from the original owner.

d) Unresolved Future Interests: If there are future interests in the property, and the holders of those interests have not agreed to the sale, the title is unmarketable. For example, if the property is subject to a life estate and the remainder interest holder has not approved the sale, the buyer could face future disputes.

e) Significant Physical Defects (Incurable Encroachments): If there is an incurable encroachment on the property, such as a neighbor's building extending onto the land, this may render the title unmarketable.

4) Waiver of Defects

Buyers can agree to waive certain defects in the contract. If the buyer knowingly agrees to purchase the property with existing encumbrances or defects, they cannot later claim the title was unmarketable.

5) Remedies for Unmarketable Title

If the seller cannot deliver marketable title, the buyer has several remedies:

a) Rescission: The buyer can rescind the contract and recover any payments made.

b) Sue for Breach: The buyer can sue the seller for breach of contract if the seller fails to deliver marketable title.

c) Specific Performance with Abatement: The buyer can seek specific performance to complete the transaction but with an abatement or reduction of the purchase price to reflect the defect in title.

Timing: Typically, these remedies are only available at or after the date of closing since the seller has until closing to correct title defects.

토지 매매에서, 계약서에 달리 명시되지 않는 한 일반적으로 상품성 있는 소유권의 묵시적 약정이 존재한다.

1) 상품성 있는 소유권(Marketable Title)

상품성 있는 소유권은 소송에 대한 불합리한 위험이 없는 소유권을 의미한다. 매도인은 일반적으로 거래종결(closing) 시에 상품성 있는 소유권을 제공해야 하며, 이는 소유권이 매수인을 미래의 법적 분쟁에 노출시킬 수 있는 부담이나 하자가 없어야 함을 의미한다.

2) 통합의 원칙(Merger Doctrine)

증서(deed)가 전달되면, 계약의 조건은 증서와 통합된다. 이 통합 후에는,

매수인은 증서에 그 조건이 명시적으로 포함되지 않는 한 토지 매매계약의 조항의 이행을 더 이상 강제할 수 없다.

3) 소유권을 상품성 없게 만드는 하자(Defects That Make Title Unmarketable)

다음과 같은 사항들이 소유권을 상품성이 없게 만들 수 있다.

a) 사적 부담(Private Encumbrances): 저당권(mortgages), 약정(covenants), 옵션(options), 지역권(easements)과 같은 사적 부담이 있는 소유권은 매수인이 이러한 부담을 수락하기로 명시적으로 동의하지 않는 한 상품성이 없다.

b) 토지용도규제 위반(Zoning Violations): 토지가 토지용도규제 규정을 위반하고 있는 경우, 소유권은 상품성 없는 것으로 간주될 수 있다. 그러나 단순히 토지용도규제법의 적용을 받는 것만으로는 상품성에 영향을 미치지는 않는다.

c) 확정되지 않은 취득시효에 의한 소유권(Title Acquired by Adverse Possession Not Quieted): 매도인의 소유권이 취득시효를 통해 획득되었지만, 소유권 확인 소송(quiet title action)을 통해 공식적으로 확정되지 않은 경우, 원소유권자의 클레임 제기 위험 때문에 소유권은 상품성이 없는 것으로 간주된다.

d) 해결되지 않은 미래의 권리(Unresolved Future Interests): 토지에 미래의 권리가 있고, 그 미래의 권리의 보유자가 토지 매도에 동의하지 않은 경우, 소유권은 상품성이 없게 된다. 예를 들어, 토지가 종신소유권(life estate)의 대상이고 잔여권자(remainder interest holder)가 매도를 승인하지 않은 경우, 매수인은 미래의 분쟁에 직면할 수 있기 때문에 이런 경우 소유권은 상품성이 없게 된다.

e) 중대한 물리적 하자(Significant Physical Defects): 이웃의 건물이 토지에 걸쳐 있는 것과 같이 치유 불가능한 침범이 있는 경우, 이는 소유권을 상품성 없게 만들 수 있다.

4) 하자에 대한 포기(Waiver of Defects)

매수인은 계약에서 특정의 하자에 대한 포기를 할 수 있다. 매수인이 토지에 부담이나 하자가 있는 것을 알면서 매수하기로 알고 동의한 경우에는 이후에 소유권이 상품성 없다고 주장할 수 없다.

5) 상품성 없는 소유권에 대한 구제책(Remedies for Unmarketable Title)

매도인이 상품성 있는 소유권을 제공할 수 없는 경우, 매수인은 다음과 같은 구제책을 가진다.

a) 해제(Rescission): 매수인은 계약을 해제하고 이미 지급한 금액을 회수할 수 있다.

b) 계약 위반 소송(Sue for Breach): 매도인이 상품성 있는 소유권을 제공하지 못하면, 매수인은 매도인을 계약 위반으로 소송할 수 있다.

c) 가격 조정을 통한 특정 이행(Specific Performance with Abatement): 매수인은 소유권의 하자를 반영하여 매수 가격의 감액을 요구하면서 거래 완료를 위한 특정 이행 청구를 할 수 있다.

시기(Timing): 일반적으로 이러한 구제책은 매도인이 소유권 하자를 수정할 수 있는 거래종결 또는 그 이후에만 사용이 가능하다.

4. 거주적합성에 대한 묵시적 보증 (Implied Warranty of Fitness or Suitability (New Homes))

This warranty assures the buyer that the home is constructed with adequate materials and workmanship, ensuring its habitability and suitability for living. This warranty typically covers latent defects - defects that cannot be discovered through a reasonable inspection, such as faulty electrical systems, plumbing issues, or a leaky roof.

Timing: Claims for breach of this warranty must be brought within a reasonable time after discovering the defect. In some jurisdictions, a statutory period of one to ten years is specified, depending on the nature of the defect (e.g., structural or foundational defects).

Disclaimer and Waiver: The implied warranty can be disclaimed by the builder or waived by the buyer, but the disclaimer must be clear and unambiguous. A general disclaimer such as "property sold as is" is typically insufficient to waive the warranty.

Example: Jane buys a newly constructed home from a developer. A few months after moving in, Jane notices that the roof leaks during heavy rains, which causes water damage inside the house. The leak was not noticeable at the time of sale and could not have been discovered through a reasonable inspection. Jane can file a claim under the implied warranty of fitness because the defect (a leaky roof) is a latent construction defect, which is covered under the warranty.

거주적합성에 대한 묵시적 보증은 매수인에게 주택이 적절한 자재와 공사로 건축되었으며, 거주 가능성과 생활에 적합함을 보장하는 것이다. 이 보증은 일반적으로 합리적인 검사로 발견할 수 없는 잠재적 하자(latent defects)를 포함하며, 예를 들어 하자 있는 전기 시스템, 배관 문제 또는 누수 지붕 등이 있다.

시기(Timing): 거주적합성에 대한 묵시적 보증 위반에 대한 청구는 하자를 발견한 후 합리적인 기간 내에 제기되어야 한다. 일부 관할권에서는 하자의 성격(예: 구조적 또는 기초적 하자)에 따라 1년에서 10년까지의 법정 기간이 지정되어 있다.

면책 및 포기(Disclaimer and Waiver): 이 묵시적 보증은 건설업자에 의해 면책되거나 매수인에 의해 포기될 수 있지만, 면책 조항은 명확하고 모호하지 않아야 한다. "현 상태로(as is)" 매도와 같은 일반적인 면책 조항은 이 보증을 포기하기에 일반적으로 충분하지 않다.

예시: 제인은 개발업자로부터 신축 주택을 매수한다. 입주 후 몇 달 후, 제인은

폭우 시 지붕에서 누수가 발생하여 집 내부에 물 피해를 입는 것을 발견한다. 누수는 주택 매도 시점에 눈에 띄지 않았으며, 합리적인 검사로 발견될 수 없었다. 제인은 거주적합성에 대한 묵시적 보증에 따라 청구를 제기할 수 있다.

5. 공개의무(Disclosure Duty)

In many jurisdictions, sellers have a legal duty to disclose known material physical defects in a property to the buyer. This duty is designed to protect buyers from hidden defects that could affect the property's value, safety, or desirability.

A defect is considered material if it substantially affects the value of the property, health or safety of residents, or the desirability of the property to a buyer.

If the seller fails to disclose a material defect, the buyer may have the option to rescind the sale or seek damages.

Example: Sarah sells her home to Adam. Sarah is aware of a serious mold problem behind the walls, caused by poor ventilation in the bathrooms. The mold is not visible during Adam's inspection, and Sarah does not disclose it. Adam later finds the mold and sues Sarah for fraudulent concealment, as the mold problem affects the health of the residents and substantially decreases the home's value. Sarah cannot escape liability by saying the home was sold "as is."

많은 관할권에서, 매도인은 매수인에게 부동산의 알려진 중요한 물리적 하자를 공개할 법적 의무가 있다. 이 의무는 부동산의 가치, 안전 또는 매력에 영향을 줄 수 있는 숨겨진 하자로부터 매수인을 보호하기 위해 고안되었다.

부동산의 가치, 거주자의 건강 또는 안전 또는 매수인에게 부동산의 매력에 실질적으로 영향을 미치는 경우에 하자는 중요한(material) 하자로 간주된다.

매도인이 중요한 하자를 공개하지 않은 경우, 매수인은 매매를 해제하거나 손해배상을 청구할 수 있다.

예시: 사라는 애덤에게 집을 판다. 사라는 욕실의 환기 불량으로 인해 벽 뒤에 심각한 곰팡이 문제가 있다는 것을 알고 있다. 곰팡이는 애덤의 검사 중에 보이지 않았으며, 사라는 이를 공개하지 않았다. 애덤은 나중에 곰팡이를 발견하고 사라를 사기적 은폐로 소송을 제기한다. 곰팡이 문제는 거주자의 건강에 영향을 미치며 집의 가치를 상당히 감소시킨다. 사라는 집을 "현 상태로(as is)" 매도했다고 말함으로써 책임을 피할 수 없다.

6. 형평법적 전환(Equitable Conversion)

The doctrine of equitable conversion governs the transfer of interests in real property once a land sale contract is signed. While the seller retains legal title during the period between contract execution and closing, equitable title passes to the buyer upon signing the contract. This means the buyer is viewed as the equitable owner of the property, and the seller essentially holds the property in trust for the buyer until the closing.

1) Risk of Loss

Under the doctrine of equitable conversion, the risk of loss (e.g., property damage) generally shifts to the buyer as soon as the contract is executed, even if the buyer has not yet taken possession of the property.

Majority Rule: The buyer bears the risk of loss between signing the contract and closing, even if the property is damaged before they take possession. The only exception is if the loss is caused by the seller's intentional or negligent actions.

Uniform Vendor and Purchaser Risk Act (Minority Rule): In some jurisdictions, the seller retains the risk of loss until the buyer takes possession or title is transferred. Under this Act, if a material part of the property is destroyed before the title transfer or the buyer's possession, the seller bears the risk.

Example (Majority Rule): Bob signs a contract to buy Sarah's house. A week later, a storm damages the roof, but the closing hasn't happened yet. Under the majority rule, Bob would bear the cost of repairs, even though he hasn't moved in.

Example (Uniform Vendor and Purchaser Risk Act): In a jurisdiction following the Act, Sarah would bear the cost of repairs because Bob hasn't taken possession, and the title hasn't been transferred.

2) Action Against the Seller

If a legal claim arises against the seller based on events that occurred before the execution of the contract, a judgment obtained after the contract is not enforceable against the property itself. Instead, the seller's interest is now considered to be in the sale proceeds, rather than the real property.

Example: If a creditor obtains a judgment against the seller for a pre-contract debt after the contract is signed, that judgment cannot be enforced against the property because the seller's interest has already been converted into a right to the sale proceeds.

형평법적 전환(equitable conversion)의 원칙은 토지 매매계약이 체결된 후 부동산에 대한 권리의 이전을 규율한다. 계약 체결과 거래종결 사이의 기간 동안 매도인은 법적 소유권을 보유하지만, 계약 서명 시에 형평법상의 소유권(equitable title)은 매수인에게 이전된다. 이는 매수인이 부동산의 형평법상 소유권자로 간주되며, 매도인은 거래종결까지 부동산을 매수인을 위해 신탁이 설정된 것으로 본다는 것을 의미한다.

1) 위험의 이전(Risk of Loss)

형평법적 전환의 원칙에 따라, 위험(예: 부동산에 대한 손상)은 일반적으로 계약이 체결되면 매수인에게 이전된다. 이는 매수인이 아직 부동산을 점유하지 않았더라도 적용된다.

다수의견(Majority Rule): 계약과 거래종결 사이에 매수인은 위험을 부담하며, 부동산에 손상이 발생해도 매수인이 비용을 부담한다. 단, 손해가 매도인의 고의 또는 과실로 인한 경우는 예외이다.

통일 매도인 및 매수인 위험법(Uniform Vendor and Purchaser Risk Act, 소수의견): 일부 관할권에서는 매수인이 부동산을 점유하거나 소유권이 이전될 때까지 매도인이 위험을 부담한다. 이 법에 따르면, 소유권 이전이나 매수인의 점유 이전에 부동산의 중요한 부분이 파괴된 경우, 매도인이 위험을 부담하게 된다.

예시(다수의견): 밥이 사라의 집을 매수하기로 계약을 체결한다. 일주일 후, 폭풍으로 지붕이 손상되었지만 거래종결은 아직 이루어지지 않았다. 다수의견에 따르면, 밥은 수리 비용을 부담해야 하며, 밥이 아직 점유하지 않았더라도 동일하다.

예시(통일 매도인 및 매수인 위험법 적용 시): 통일 매도인 및 매수인 위험법을 따르는 관할권에서는, 밥이 아직 점유하지 않았고 소유권이 이전되지 않았으므로 사라가 수리 비용을 부담해야 한다.

2) 매도인에 대한 소송(Action Against the Seller)

계약 체결 전에 발생한 사건에 기반하여 매도인에 대한 법적 청구가 발생한 경우, 계약 체결 후에 얻은 판결은 부동산 자체에 대해 집행될 수 없다. 대신, 매도인의 권리는 이제 부동산이 아닌 매도 대금에 있는 것으로 간주된다.

예시: 채권자가 계약 체결 후에 매도인의 계약 전 부채에 대한 판결을 얻은 경우, 매도인의 권리는 이미 매도 대금에 대한 권리로 전환되었으므로 그 판결은 부동산에 대해 집행될 수 없다.

B 거래종결(Closing)

In real estate transactions, the closing is the final step where legal ownership of the property is transferred from the seller (grantor) to the buyer (grantee). This transfer is effectuated through the delivery of a deed, a legal instrument that documents and formalizes the change in ownership. For the transfer to be valid, certain requirements must be met, including intent (delivery of the deed), acceptance by the grantee, and compliance with the Statute of Frauds.

부동산 거래에서 거래종결(closing)은 매도인(양도인)으로부터 매수인(양수인)에게 부동산의 법적 소유권이 이전되는 최종 단계이다. 소유권의 이전은 소유권의 변경을 문서화하고 공식화하는 법적 문서인 증서(deed)의 전달을 통해 이루어진다. 소유권의 이전이 유효하려면, 소유권 이전에 대한 의사(증서의 전달), 양수인의 수락과 사기방지법의 준수를 포함한 특정 요건들이 충족되어야 한다.

1. 소유권 이전 의사(Intent to Transfer - Delivery of Deed)

For a transfer of real property to be effective, the grantor must demonstrate intent to make a present transfer of the property interest to the grantee. This intent is a critical element in real estate transactions, and it is often evidenced by the delivery of the deed. However, physical delivery of the deed is not always required; instead, the grantor's words and actions can establish the necessary intent.

부동산의 이전이 효력을 가지려면, 양도인은 양수인에게 부동산 권리를 현재 이전하려는 의사를 표시하여야 한다. 이러한 소유권 이전의 의사는 부동산 거래에서 중요한 요소이며, 종종 증서의 전달로 증명된다. 그러나 증서의 물리적 전달이 항상 필요한 것은 아니며, 대신 양도인의 말과 행위가 필요한 의사를 입증할 수 있다.

1) 양도인의 증서 보유(Retention of Deed by Grantor)

When the grantor keeps the deed, there is no presumption of intent to transfer the property. In such cases, parol evidence (oral testimony) can be used to determine whether the grantor intended to make a present transfer.

Example: A parent creates a deed transferring property to their child but keeps the deed in a drawer. Without other evidence of intent to transfer, this alone does not establish a present transfer of the property.

양도인이 증서를 보유하고 있는 경우, 소유권 이전의 의사는 추정되지 않는다. 이러한 경우, 구두 증거(parol evidence)를 사용하여 양도인이 현재 소유권을 이전하려는 의사가 있었는지 결정할 수 있다.

예시: 부모가 자녀에게 부동산을 이전하는 증서를 작성하지만, 그 증서를 서랍에 보관하고 있다. 소유권 이전에 대한 다른 증거가 없다면, 이것만으로는 부동산의 현재의 이전을 확립하지 못한다.

2) 양수인에 대한 증서 전달(Transfer of Deed to Grantee)

When the grantor transfers the deed directly to the grantee, there is a presumption that the grantor intended to make a present transfer. While parol evidence can be used to rebut this presumption (such as when the grantor intended only to create a mortgage), oral conditions (conditions not stated in the deed) are generally unenforceable.

Example: A grantor hands a deed to a grantee, stating orally, "I'll give you the property if you get married." Since the condition does not appear in the deed, the condition is unenforceable, and the deed transfer is considered valid.

양도인이 증서를 직접 양수인에게 전달하는 경우, 양도인이 현재 소유권을 이전하려는 의사가 있었다는 추정이 있게 된다. 구두 증거를 사용하여 이 추정을 반박할 수 있지만(예: 양도인이 단지 저당권을 설정하려고 했을 때), 증서에 명시되지 않은 구두 조건은 일반적으로 집행될 수 없다.

예시: 양도인이 증서를 양수인에게 건네며 구두로 "네가 결혼하면 이 부동산을 줄게"라고 말한다. 조건이 증서에 명시되어 있지 않으므로, 그 구두조건은 집행될 수 없으며 증서 이전은 유효한 것으로 간주된다.

3) 제3자에 대한 증서 전달(Transfer of Deed to a Third Party)

a) Grantor's Agent

If the grantor transfers the deed to their own agent (e.g., an attorney) with instructions to deliver it later, it is treated as if the grantor still retains control of the deed. The grantor can recall the deed before it is delivered to the grantee, meaning no present transfer has occurred until the agent delivers the deed.

b) Grantee's Agent

If the deed is transferred to the grantee's agent, it is treated as if the deed has been transferred directly to the grantee, and the intent to transfer is presumed.

c) Independent Agent

When the deed is given to a third party (e.g., an escrow agent) as part of a real estate contract, the agent must release the deed to the buyer when certain conditions (such as payment) are met. Until the conditions are satisfied, the seller retains title to the property.

Retrieval by Grantor: If there is a written contract, the grantor cannot recall the deed from the escrow agent before the condition fails. However, if the contract is oral, the grantor may reclaim the deed because the Statute of Frauds requires a written contract for land sale contracts to be enforceable.

Time of Transfer: Once the condition is satisfied (e.g., full payment), title automatically vests in the buyer. The date of transfer may "relate back" to the date the deed was placed in escrow, especially if the grantor dies or becomes incapacitated before the condition is met.

a) 양도인의 대리인(Grantor's Agent)

양도인이 자신의 대리인(예: 변호사)에게 증서를 전달하고 나중에 전달하도록 지시한 경우, 이는 양도인이 여전히 증서의 통제권을 유지하는 것으로 간주된다. 양도인은 증서가 양수인에게 전달되기 전에 증서를 회수할 수 있으므로, 대리인이 증서를 전달할 때까지 현재 소유권 이전이 발생하지 않는다.

b) 양수인의 대리인(Grantee's Agent)

증서가 양수인의 대리인에게 전달된 경우, 이는 증서가 직접 양수인에게 전달된 것으로 간주되며, 소유권을 이전하려는 의사가 있는 것으로 추정된다.

c) 독립 대리인(Independent Agent)

증서가 부동산 계약의 일환으로 제3자(예: 에스크로 대리인)에게 주어졌을 때, 대리인은 특정 조건(예: 지불)이 충족되면 증서를 매수인에게 전달해야 한다. 조건이 충족될 때까지 매도인은 부동산의 소유권을 유지한다.

양도인의 회수(Retrieval by Grantor): 서면 계약이 있는 경우, 양도인은 조건이 실패하기 전에 에스크로 대리인으로부터 증서를 회수할 수 없다. 그러나 계약이 구두인 경우, 양도인은 증서를 회수할 수 있다. 이는 사기방지법이 토지 매매계약의 집행을 위해 서면 계약을 요구하기 때문이다.

이전 시점(Time of Transfer): 조건이 충족되면(예: 전액 지불), 소유권은 자동으로 매수인에게 귀속된다. 이전의 날짜는 증서가 에스크로에 놓인 날짜로 "소급(relate back)"될 수 있으며, 특히 양도인이 조건이 충족되기 전에 사망하거나 무능력해진 경우 그렇다.

4) 양수인의 수락(Grantee's Acceptance)

For a real property transfer to be complete, the grantee must accept the deed. Even if the grantor delivers the deed with intent to transfer, the transfer is not legally effective unless and until the grantee accepts it.

a) Presumption of Acceptance

Grantee's acceptance is presumed if the deed conveys a beneficial interest to the grantee. This means that unless there is evidence to the contrary, it is assumed that the grantee has accepted the deed because owning property is generally considered beneficial.

b) Relation Back Doctrine

When acceptance is made, it can relate back to the date when the grantor initially delivered the deed (e.g., to an escrow agent). This is significant because it ensures that the transfer is valid even if the grantor's circumstances change between the delivery and the formal acceptance.

Example: A delivers a deed to an escrow agent, instructing the agent to give the deed to B once B completes the payment. A dies before the payment is made, but B later makes the payment and accepts the deed. Acceptance relates back to the date when A delivered the deed to the escrow agent, making the transfer valid.

c) Rejection of Deed

If the grantee rejects the deed, no title passes, and the grantor retains ownership. Rejection can be made verbally or through actions that indicate refusal to take ownership of the property.

d) Effect of Post-Acceptance Change of Mind

Once the grantee accepts the deed, the transfer of ownership is legally complete. If the grantee changes their mind after acceptance, simply returning or canceling the deed is ineffective to undo the transfer.

To transfer the property back to the original grantor (or to anyone else), a new, valid deed must be executed by the grantee. This new deed must meet all the formal requirements of a valid deed (e.g., written document, identification of the parties and property, intent to transfer, and signature).

Example: A grants a deed to B, and B accepts it. Five minutes later, B decides he no longer wants the property and hands the deed back to A. This act does not transfer the property back to A. For A to regain ownership, B must execute a new deed transferring the property to A.

부동산의 소유권 이전이 완료되려면, 양수인이 증서를 수락해야 한다. 양도인이 소유권 이전의 의사로 증서를 전달하더라도, 양수인이 이를 수락하지 않으면 소유권 이전은 법적으로 효력이 없다.

a) 수락의 추정(Presumption of Acceptance)

증서가 양수인에게 수익적 권리를 부여하는 경우, 양수인의 수락은 추정된다. 이는 반대의 증거가 없는 한, 부동산 소유는 일반적으로 이익이 되므로 양수인이 증서를 수락했다고 간주되는 것으로 해석된다.

b) 소급 적용 원칙(Relation Back Doctrine)

수락이 이루어지면, 이는 양도인이 처음으로 증서를 전달한 날짜에 소급하여 효력이 발생할 수 있다. 이는 증서 전달과 공식적인 수락 사이에 양도인의 상황이 변하더라도 이전이 유효함을 보장하기 때문에 중요한 의

미를 갖는다.

예시: A는 에스크로 대리인에게 증서를 전달하며, B가 대금을 완불하면 증서를 전달하라고 지시한다. A는 대금이 지불되기 전에 사망하지만, B는 나중에 대금을 지불하고 증서를 수락한다. 수락은 A가 에스크로 대리인에게 증서를 전달한 날짜로 소급되므로, 소유권 이전은 유효하다.

c) 증서의 거절(Rejection of Deed)

양수인이 증서의 수락을 거절하면, 소유권은 이전되지 않으며 양도인이 소유권을 계속 보유하게 된다. 거절은 구두로 또는 재산의 소유권을 취득하는 것을 거절하는 행위를 통해 이루어질 수 있다.

d) 수락 후 마음이 변한 경우의 효과(Effect of Post-Acceptance Change of Mind)

양수인이 증서를 수락하면, 소유권의 이전은 법적으로 완료된다. 수락 후에 양수인이 마음을 바꾸더라도, 단순히 증서를 반환하거나 취소하는 것으로는 소유권 이전을 취소할 수 없다.

재산의 소유권을 원양도인(또는 다른 사람)에게 다시 이전하려면, 양수인이 새로운 유효한 증서를 작성해야 한다. 이 새로운 증서는 유효한 증서의 모든 형식적 요건들(예: 서면 문서, 당사자 및 재산의 식별, 소유권 이전의 의사, 서명)을 충족해야 한다.

예시: A가 B에게 증서를 전달하고, B가 이를 수락한다. 5분 후, B는 더 이상 재산을 원하지 않기로 결정하고 증서를 A에게 돌려준다. 이 행위는 재산의 소유권을 A에게 다시 이전하지 않는다. A가 소유권을 되찾으려면, B가 재산의 소유권을 A에게 이전하는 새로운 증서를 작성해야 한다.

C 유효한 증서(Valid Deed)

A deed is the legal document used to transfer ownership of real property from the grantor to the grantee. To be legally effective, a deed must meet several requirements to be considered valid. It must comply with the Statute of Frauds, which mandates that real estate transfers be in writing and contain material terms. Unlike contracts, consideration is not required for a valid deed, making it different from other types of legal agreements.

증서(deed)는 양도인으로부터 양수인에게 부동산의 소유권을 이전하는 데 사용되는 법적 문서이다. 법적으로 효력을 가지려면, 증서는 유효한 것으로 간주되기 위해 여러 가지 요건을 충족해야 한다. 사기방지법(statute of frauds)을 준수해야 하며, 부동산의 소유권 이전은 서면으로 작성되고 중요 조건을 포함해야 한다. 일반적인 다른 계약과는 달리, 유효한 증서에는 약인(consideration)이 요구되지 않는다.

1. 당사자(Parties)

The grantor (the party transferring the interest) and the grantee (the party receiving the interest) must be clearly identified in the deed. The deed must be signed by the grantor. While it is customary in some states to have the deed witnessed or notarized, it is not required in most jurisdictions. The grantee does not need to sign the deed for it to be valid.

Example: A grantor executes a deed conveying "Blackacre to my neighbors." Unless extrinsic evidence identifies who the "neighbors" are, the deed is ineffective and has no legal force.

양도인과 양수인은 증서에서 명확하게 명시되어야 한다. 증서는 양도인이 서명해야 한다. 일부 주에서는 증서에 증인이나 공증인의 인증을 받는 것이 관례이지만, 대부분의 관할권에서는 요구되지는 않는다. 양수인은 증서가 유효하기 위해 반드시 서명할 필요가 없다.

예시: 양도인이 "토지를 이웃들에게"라고 명시한 증서를 작성한다. 이웃들이 누구인지 외부 증거(extrinsic evidence)로 식별되지 않는 한, 이 증서는 효력이 없으며 법적 구속력이 없다.

2. 소유권 이전의 문구(Words of Transfer)

The deed must contain language indicating the grantor's present intent to transfer the property interest to the grantee. This section of the deed is known as the granting clause.

Example: A deed stating, "I transfer Blackacre to B" is sufficient, as it clearly indicates the present intent to transfer ownership.

증서는 양도인이 양수인에게 부동산 소유권의 권리를 현재 이전하려는 의도를 나타내는 문구를 포함해야 한다. 증서의 이 부분을 양도 조항(granting clause)이라고 한다.

예시: "나는 토지를 B에게 이전한다"는 내용의 증서는 소유권을 현재 이전하려는 의도를 명확히 나타내고 있으므로 소유권 이전의 문구로서 충분하다.

3. 부동산의 설명(Description of the Property)

The deed must reasonably describe the property being conveyed so that it can be identified with certainty. The description does not need to be exact, but it must be sufficient to distinguish the property from other properties.

증서는 이전되는 부동산을 합리적으로 식별할 수 있도록 설명해야 한다. 설명은 정확할 필요는 없지만, 해당 부동산을 다른 부동산과 구별할 수 있을 정도로 충분해야 한다.

4. 약인 미요구(No Consideration)

Unlike contracts, consideration (something of value exchanged between parties) is not required for a deed to be valid. The deed is still effective whether the transfer is made as a gift or for value.

계약과 달리, 증서가 유효하기 위해서는 약인(consideration)(당사자 간에 교환되는 가치 있는 것)이 필요하지 않다. 이전이 증여이든 대가를 지급하고 받는 것이든, 증서는 여전히 효력이 있다.

D 등록법(Recording Act)

The Recording Act determines the priority of rights between parties claiming an interest in the same real property. The act establishes the legal framework for recording deeds, mortgages, and other instruments, and governs how these documents affect property rights. While a deed does not need to be recorded to be valid between the grantor and grantee, recording provides public notice and helps protect the grantee's rights against subsequent purchasers or creditors.

등록법은 동일한 부동산에 대한 권리를 주장하는 당사자들 사이의 권리의 우선순위를 결정한다. 이 법은 증서(deeds), 저당권(mortgages) 및 기타 문서를 등록하는 법적 체계를 수립하고, 이러한 문서들이 부동산 권리에 어떻게 영향을 미치는지를 규율한다. 증서는 양도인과 양수인 간의 소유권 이전이 유효하기 위해 등록될 필요는 없지만, 등록은 공적 통지를 제공하며 양수인의 권리를 이후의 매수인이나 채권자로부터 보호하는 데 도움이 된다.

1. 등록법의 유형(Types of Recording Statutes)

There are three types of recording statutes: Notice, Race, and Race-Notice statutes. Each operates differently in determining which party prevails when there are conflicting property claims.

등록법에는 세 가지 유형이 있다. 즉, 통지법(Notices Statutes), 선등록법(Race Statutes) 및 선등록통지법 (Race-Notice Statutes)이 있다. 각각은 부동산에 대한 권리가 충돌할 때 어느 당사자가 우선하는지를 결정하는 방식이 다르다.

1) 통지법(Notice Statute)

Under a notice statute, a subsequent purchaser who purchases for value without notice of a prior unrecorded interest prevails over an ealier grantee who failed to record. Notice statutes protect good faith purchasers who have no knowledge of a prior unrecorded interest.

Example of a Notice Statute: "No conveyance or mortgage of real property shall be good against subsequent purchasers for value and without notice unless the same be recorded according to law."

Example: O conveys Blackacre to A on January 1, and A does not record. O then conveys Blackacre to B on January 15, and B has no knowledge of A's deed. Even if A records later, B, as a bona fide purchaser without notice, wins under a notice statute.

통지법(notice statute)에서는 소유권 이전에 등록되지 않은 권리에 대한 통지가 없는 상태에서 대가를 지불하고 부동산을 매수한 후속 매수인이 등록을 안한 이전의 양수인보다 우선한다. 통지법은 소유권 이전에 등록되지 않은 부동산의 권리를 알지 못하는 선의의 매수인(good faith purchaser)을 보호하는 것이다.

통지법의 예시: "부동산의 양도나 저당권은 법률에 따라 등록되지 않으면 대가를 지급하고 통지를 받지 않은 후속 매수인에 대하여 유효하지 않다."

예시: O가 1월 1일에 토지를 A에게 양도하지만, A는 등록하지 않는다. O는 1월 15일에 토지를 B에게 양도하며, B는 A의 증서에 대해 알지 못한다. 이후 A가 등록하더라도, 통지법 하에서는 통지가 없는 선의의 매수인인 B의 권리가 우선한다.

2) 선등록법(Race Statute)

Under a race statute, the first party to record a deed, mortgage, or other interest wins, regardless of whether they had notice of a prior unrecorded interest. This means that even if a subsequent purchaser is aware of a prior unrecorded interest, they can still take priority by recording their deed first.

Example of a Race Statute: Race statute: "No conveyance or mortgage of real property shall be good against subsequent purchasers for value unless the same be first recorded according to law."

Example: O conveys Blackacre to A on January 1, and A does not record. O then conveys Blackacre to B on January 15, and B records immediately. Under a race statute, B wins, even if B knew about A's unrecorded deed.

선등록법(race statute) 하에서는 증서나 저당권 또는 기타 권리를 먼저 등록한 당사자의 권리가 우선하며, 그들이 이전에 등록되지 않은 권리에 대한 통지가 있었는지는 중요하지 않다. 이는 후속 매수인이 이전에 등록되지 않은 권리를 알고 있더라도, 자신이 증서를 먼저 등록함으로써 우선권을 가질 수 있음을 의미한다.

선등록법의 예시: "부동산의 양도나 저당권은 법률에 따라 먼저 등록되지 않으면 대가를 지급한 후속 매수인에 대하여 유효하지 않다."

예시: O가 1월 1일에 토지를 A에게 양도하지만, A는 등록하지 않는다. O는 1월 15일에 토지를 B에게 양도하며, B는 즉시 등록한다. 선등록법 하에서는 B가 A의 등록되지 않은 증서를 알고 있었더라도 B의 권리가 우선한다.

3) 선등록통지법(Race-Notice Statute)

Under a race-notice statute, a subsequent purchaser must be a bona fide purchaser and record their interest first to take priority. This means that even if a subsequent purchaser is without notice, they must also record before the earlier grantee to have superior rights.

Example of a Race-notice statute: "No conveyance or mortgage of real property shall be good against subsequent purchasers for value and without notice who shall first record."

Example: O conveys Blackacre to A on January 1, and A does not record. O then conveys Blackacre to B on January 15. B is unaware of A's deed and records on January 16. If A records on January 17, B wins under a race-notice statute because B was without notice and recorded first.

선등록통지법(race-notice statute) 하에서는, 후속 매수인이 선의의 매수인이어야 하며, 우선권을 갖기 위해 자신의 권리를 먼저 등록해야 한다. 이는 후속 매수인이 통지를 받지 않아더라도, 우선 권리를 가지려면 이전의 양수인보다 먼저 등록해야 함을 의미한다.

선등록통지법의 예시: "부동산의 양도나 저당권은 대가를 지급하고 통지를 받고 먼저 등록을 한 후속 매수인에 대하여 유효하지 않다."

예시: O가 1월 1일에 토지를 A에게 양도하지만, A는 등록하지 않는다. O는

1월 15일에 토지를 B에게 양도한다. B는 A의 증서에 대해 알지 못하며, 1월 16일에 등록한다. A가 1월 17일에 등록하는 경우, 선등록통지법 하에서는 B가 통지가 없었고 먼저 등록했으므로 B가 우선한다.

2. 대가의 지급(Paid Value)

To be protected under the recording acts, a subsequent purchaser must have paid value for the interest.

1) Mortgagees

A mortgagee who receives a mortgage in exchange for a loan is considered to have paid value and is protected under the recording acts. However, if the mortgage is given without consideration (e.g., a gift), it does not qualify.

2) Judgment Liens

Creditors who obtain judgment liens are generally protected against subsequent claims if the lien is recorded before other interests arise.

3) Donees and Heirs

These parties are not protected against subsequent purchasers for value, even if they record first.

4) Shelter Rule

A grantee who receives property from a bona fide purchaser (BFP) "shelters" under the BFP's status, even if the grantee would not otherwise qualify as a BFP.

Example: A sells Blackacre to B, a BFP who records. B later sells Blackacre to C, a donee. Because B was protected, C takes shelter under B's status and is protected as well.

등록법에 따라 보호받으려면, 후속 매수인은 그 권리에 대해 대가를 지급해야 한다.

1) 저당권자 (Mortgagees)

대출에 대한 대가로 저당권을 받은 저당권자는 대가를 지급한 것으로 간주되며, 등록법에 따라 보호받는다. 그러나 저당권이 대가 없이 주어진 경우(예: 무상제공)에는 이는 해당되지 않는다.

2) 판결 담보권자 (Judgment Liens)

판결 담보권을 얻은 채권자는 일반적으로 그 담보권이 다른 권리가 발생하기 전에 등록되었다면 이후의 청구로부터 보호받는다.

3) 무상수령자와 상속인 (Donees and Heirs)

무상수령자와 상속인은 먼저 등록하더라도 대가를 지급한 후속 매수인에 대하여 보호받지 못한다.

4) 은신처 원칙 (Shelter Rule)

선의의 매수인으로부터 부동산을 받은 양수인은, 자신이 선의의 매수인으로 자격을 갖추지 못하더라도 선의의 매수인 지위에 의하여 보호를 받는다.

예시: A가 토지를 등록한 선의의 매수인 B에게 매도한다. B는 나중에 토지를 무상수령자에게 제공한다. B가 선의의 매수인으로 보호를 받았으므로, C는 B의 지위에 따라 보호받는다.

3. 권원의 연결(Chain-of-Title Problems)

Chain-of-title problems arise when recorded documents, such as deeds or mortgages, are not properly connected in the public record, creating ambiguities or gaps in ownership. These problems can disrupt the transfer of good title and lead to disputes between parties who each believe they have a valid claim to the same property.

권원의 연결(chain of title) 문제는 증서나 저당권과 같은 등록된 문서가 공적 등록에서 제대로 연결되지 않아 소유권에 모호함이나 공백이 생길 때 발생한다. 이러한 문제는 올바른 소유권의 이전을 방해하고, 각자 동일한 부동산에 대해 유효한 청구를 가지고 있다고 믿는 당사자들 간의 분쟁으로 이어질 수 있다.

1) 미등록 증서(Wild Deed)

A wild deed is a deed that is outside the chain of title and does not provide notice to subsequent purchasers because it cannot be found by a reasonable title search. Even though the wild deed is technically recorded, it is not discoverable in a standard title search, and thus it does not provide constructive notice to subsequent purchasers.

Example: O owns Blackacre. O sells Blackacre to A. A does not record the deed from O to A. A sells Blackacre to B. B records the deed from A to B. O sells Blackacre to C. C records the deed from O to C.

- Notice Statute: C is a BFP because B paid value for Blackacre. C had no actual or constructive notice of A's or B's interests. B's deed is a wild deed and does not provide constructive notice to C because it is outside the chain of title. C prevails over B. C holds valid title to Blackacre.

- Race Statute: B recorded the deed from A to B before C recorded the deed from O to C. However, B's deed is a wild deed since the deed from O to A was unrecorded, B's recorded deed from A to B is disconnected from the chain of title. B's recording is ineffective against subsequent purchasers who rely on the chain of title. C recorded after B, but within the proper chain of title. Despite B recording first, C prevails because B's wild deed does not impart constructive notice, and C's deed is the first recorded within the chain of title. C holds valid title to Blackacre.

- Race-Notice Statute: C is a BFP without notice. B recorded before C, but B's deed is a wild deed outside the chain of title. C recorded after B, but within the proper chain of title from O. C prevails because C had no notice of B's interest. C recorded within the chain of title. B's prior recording is ineffective due to being a wild deed. C holds valid title to Blackacre.

미등록 증서(wild deed)는 권원 연결 밖에 있는 증서로, 합리적인 소유권 조사로는 찾을 수 없기 때문에 후속 매수인에게 통지를 제공하지 못한다. 미등록 증서는 등록되어 있다 하더라도, 합리적인 소유권 조사에서는 발견될 수 없으므로 후속 매수인에게 의제 통지를 제공하지 않는다.

예시: 토지를 소유하고 있는 O는 토지를 A에게 매도한다. A는 O에서 A로의 증서를 등록하지 않는다. A는 토지를 B에게 매도한다. B는 A에서 B로의 증서를 등록한다. O는 토지를 C에게 매도한다. C는 O에서 C로의 증서를 등록한다.

- 통지법(Notice Statute): C는 토지에 대해 대가를 지급한 선의의 매수인이다. C는 A나 B의 권리에 대한 실제 또는 의제 통지가 없다. B의 증서는 미등록 증서며, 권원 연결 밖에 있으므로 C에게 의제 통지를 제공하지 않는다. 따라서 C는 B보다 우선하며, 부동산에 대한 유효한 소유권을 가진다.
- 선등록법(Race Statute): B는 C가 O에서 C로의 증서를 등록하기 전에 A에서 B로의 증서를 등록했다. 그러나 B의 증서는 미등록 증서로, O에서 A로의 증서가 등록되지 않아 B의 A에서 B로의 등록된 증서는 권원 연결과 연결되지 않는다. B의 등록은 권원 연결에 의존하는 후속 매수인에 대해 효력이 없다. C는 B 이후에 등록했지만, 올바른 권원 연결 내에서 등록했다. B가 먼저 등록했더라도, B의 미등록 증서는 의제 통지를 제공하지 않으므로 C의 권리가 우선한다. C는 토지에 대한 유효한 소유권을 가진다.

- 선등록통지법(Race-Notice Statute): C는 통지가 없는 선의의 매수인이다. B는 C보다 먼저 등록했지만, B의 증서는 권원 연결 밖에 있는 미등록 증서다. C는 B 이후에 등록했지만, O로부터의 올바른 권원 연결 내에서 등록했다. C는 B의 권리에 대한 통지가 없었고, 권원 연결 내에서 등록했으므로 C의 권리가 우선한다. B의 이전 등록은 미등록 증서로 인해 효력이 없다. C는 토지에 대한 유효한 소유권을 가진다.

2) 증서에 의한 금반언(Estoppel by Deed)

The estoppel by deed (After-Acquired Title) doctrine applies when a grantor conveys a property interest that the grantor does not yet own, but later acquires. The grantor is estopped (prevented) from denying the validity of the earlier conveyance once they acquire the property. Thus, title automatically passes to the earlier grantee.

Example: G, who does not own Blackacre, conveys Blackacre to A by warranty deed. G later acquires title to Blackacre from O. G sells Blackacre to B, a bona fide purchaser. B records. A sues B for title to Blackacre.

- G and A: Under the estoppel by deed doctrine, when G acquires title to Blackacre from O, that title automatically passes to A because G is estopped from denying A's rights under the earlier warranty deed. However, in notice and race-notice jurisdictions, B's subsequent purchase and recording will prevail over A.
- Notice Statute: B prevails because B had no notice of A.
- Race Statute: B prevails if B records before A.
- Race-Notice Statute: B prevails because B recorded first and had no notice of A.

증서에 의한 금반언(estoppel by deed) 또는 사후 취득 소유권(After-Acquired Title)의 원칙은 양도인이 아직 소유권이 없는 부동산의 권리를 양도한 후 나중에 소유권을 취득하는 경우에 적용된다. 양도인은 부동산을 취득하면 이전의 양도의 유효성을 부인할 수 없게 된다. 따라서 소유권은 자동으로 이전의 양수인에게 이전된다.

예시: 토지를 소유하지 않은 G가 보증 증서로 토지를 A에게 양도한다. G는 나중에 O로부터 토지의 소유권을 취득한다. G는 토지를 A의 선의의 매수인 B에게 매도한다. B는 등록한다. A는 토지의 소유권에 대해 B를 상대로 소송을 제기한다.

- G와 A 사이(G and A): 증서에 의한 금반언 원칙에 따라, G가 O로부터 토지의 소유권을 취득하면 그 소유권은 자동으로 A에게 이전된다. 이는 G가 이전의 보증 증서에 따른 A의 권리를 부인할 수 없기 때문이다. 그러나 통지법과 선등록통지법 관할권에서는 B의 이후 매수 및 등록이 A보다 우선한다.
- 통지법(Notice Statute): B는 A의 권리에 대한 통지가 없었으므로 B의 권리가 우선한다.
- 선등록법(Race Statute): B가 A보다 먼저 등록하면 B의 권리가 우선한다.
- 선등록통지법(Race-Notice Statute): B는 먼저 등록했고 A의 권리에 대한 통지가 없으므로 B의 권리가 우선한다.

4. 통지의 유형(Types of Notice)

Notice is a crucial concept under notice and race-notice statutes. There are three types of notice:

1) Actual Notice

When the purchaser actually knows of the prior interest.

Example: A tells B that he sold the property to C before selling it to B. B has actual notice of C's interest.

2) Inquiry Notice

If a reasonable investigation would have disclosed the existence of prior claims, then the grantee is deemed to possess inquiry notice.

Example: A property is occupied by someone other than the grantor. The purchaser is charged with notice of that person's potential interest.

3) Constructive Notice

Constructive notice arises from properly recorded documents. If a prior deed or mortgage is recorded, subsequent purchasers are deemed to have notice of it, even if they never actually check the records.

통지는 통지법과 선등록통지법 하에서 중요한 개념이다. 통지에는 세 가지 유형이 있다.

1) 실제 통지(Actual Notice)

매수인이 이전 권리를 사실상 알고 있는 경우이다.

예시: A가 B에게 A가 C에게 부동산을 매도한 후 B에게 매도한다고 말한다. B는 C의 권리에 대한 실제 통지를 가진다.

2) 조사 통지(Inquiry Notice)

합리적인 조사가 이전의 권리의 존재를 발견해 낼 수 있었던 경우, 양수인은 조사 통지를 가진 것으로 간주된다.[6]

예시: 부동산이 양도인이 아닌 다른 사람이 점유하고 있는 경우, 매수인은 그 사람의 잠재적 권리에 대한 통지를 가진 것으로 본다.

6) 부동산 거래 시 매수인은 일반적으로 거래 완료 전에 부동산을 조사할 의무를 부담한다. 따라서 토지 매수인이 해당 토지에 누군가가 점유하고 있는 것으로 보이는 사정이 있다면 그 토지에 대한 권리자가 있는지를 조사할 의무가 발생하며, 이를 무시하고 조사하지 않았다면 Inquiry Notice가 있었다고 간주된다. 즉, Inquiry Notice는 조사를 하면 알 수 있었던 사실에 대한 통지를 의미한다.

3) 의제 통지 (Constructive Notice)

의제 통지는 적절히 등록된 문서에서 발생한다. 양도의 증서나 저당권이 등록되어 있으면, 후속 매수인은 실제로 등록을 확인하지 않았더라도 그것에 대한 통지를 받은 것으로 간주된다.

5. 증서의 유형(Types of Deed)

Deeds are used to convey ownership of real property, and the type of deed used determines the scope of warranties and protections granted to the buyer. The three main types of deeds are General Warranty Deeds, Special Warranty Deeds, and Quitclaim Deeds. Each type offers a different level of protection for the grantee and imposes varying degrees of liability on the grantor.

증서는 부동산의 소유권을 이전하는 데 사용되며, 사용된 증서의 유형에 따라 매수인에게 부여되는 보증과 보호의 범위가 결정된다. 주요 증서의 유형은 일반 보증 증서(general warranty deed), 권리 포기 증서(quitclaim deed) 및 특정 보증 증서(special warranty deed)가 있다. 각 유형은 양수인에게 다른 수준의 보호를 제공하며, 양도인에게 다양한 정도의 책임을 부과한다.

1) 일반 보증 증서(General Warranty Deed)

A general warranty deed provides a high level of protection to the grantee by including six covenants of title - three present and three future covenants. The grantor guarantees that he holds good title to the property and will defend the grantee against any defects, even if they arose before the grantor's ownership.

1) Present Covenants

a) Covenant of Seisin: The grantor warrants that they own the property as described in the deed.

Example: If O conveys Blackacre to A but O only owns half of Blackacre, the covenant of seisin is breached.

b) Covenant of Right to Convey: The grantor warrants that they have the legal right to convey title to the property.

Example: If O is a trustee without authority to sell the trust property and conveys it to A, the covenant of the right to convey is breached.

c) Covenant Against Encumbrances: The grantor warrants that there are no encumbrances (e.g., mortgages, liens, easements) on the property not disclosed in the deed.

Example: If O conveys Blackacre to A, but there is an undisclosed easement on the property, the covenant against encumbrances is breached.

2) Future Covenants

a) Covenant of Quiet Enjoyment: The grantor warrants that the grantee's possession of the property will not be disturbed by a third party's lawful claim of title.

Example: If a third party with superior title evicts A from Blackacre, the covenant of quiet enjoyment is breached.

b) Covenant of Warranty: The grantor promises to defend the grantee against any lawful claims of superior title by others.

Example: If a third party sues A, claiming superior title, and the claim is valid, A can demand that O defend the title.

c) Covenant for Further Assurances: The grantor promises to take any further steps necessary to perfect the grantee's title if it turns out to be defective.

Example: If O needs to provide additional documentation to clear up a boundary issue, O must do so under this covenant.

일반 보증 증서(general warranty deed)는 양도인이 3개이 현재의 약정과 3개의 미래의 약정을 포함한 6가지의 약정을 양수인에게 하는 것으로 양수인에 대하여 가장 높은 수준의 보호를 제공한다. 양도인은 자신이 부동산에 대한 유효한 소유권을 가지고 있으며, 양도인의 소유권 이전에 발생한 것이라도 소유권에 대한 하자에 대해 양수인을 방어할 것을 보증하는 것이다.

1) 현재의 약정 (Present Covenants)

a) 소유권의 약정 (Covenant of Seisin): 양도인은 증서에 설명된 대로 부동산을 소유하고 있음을 보증한다.

예시: O가 토지를 A에게 양도하지만, O가 토지의 절반에만 소유권이 있는 경우, 소유권의 약정이 위반된다.

b) 양도 권리의 약정 (Covenant of Right to Convey): 양도인은 토지에 대한 소유권을 양도할 법적 권리가 있음을 보증한다.

예시: O가 신탁 재산을 매도할 권한이 없는 수탁자(trustee)임에도 불구하고 이를 A에게 양도하는 경우, 양도 권리의 약정이 위반된다.

c) 부담 부존재 약정 (Covenant Against Encumbrances): 양도인은 증서에 공개되지 않은 부동산에 대한 부담(예: 저당권, 담보권, 지역권)이 없음을 보증한다.

예시: O가 부동산을 A에게 양도하지만, 부동산에 공개되지 않은 지역권이 있는 경우, 부담 부존재 약정이 위반된다.

2) 미래의 약정 (Future Covenants)

a) 평온한 권리 향유의 약정 (Covenant of Quiet Enjoyment): 양도인은 제3자의 합법적인 소유권 청구로 인해 양수인의 부동산 점유가 방해받지 않을 것을 보증한다.

예시: 우월한 소유권을 가진 제3자가 A를 부동산에서 퇴거시키는 경우, 평온한 권리 향유의 약정이 위반된다.

a) 보증의 약정 (Covenant of Warranty): 양도인은 다른 사람의 우월

한 소유권에 대한 합법적인 청구로부터 양수인을 방어할 것을 약속한다.

예시: 제3자가 우월한 소유권을 주장하며 A를 고소하고, 그 청구가 유효한 경우, A는 O에게 소유권을 방어해 줄 것을 요구할 수 있다.

a) 추가 확인의 약정 (Covenant for Further Assurances): 양도인은 양수인의 소유권이 하자가 있는 것으로 판명될 경우, 이를 완전하게 하기 위해 필요한 추가 조치를 취할 것을 약속한다.

예시: O가 경계 문제를 해결하기 위해 추가 문서를 제공해야 하는 경우, 추가 확인의 약정에 따라 그렇게 해야 한다.

2) 권리 포기 증서(Quitclaim Deed)

A quitclaim deed provides the least protection to the grantee. The grantor makes no covenants about the quality of the title. The grantee receives only the interest that the grantor has at the time of conveyance, which could be no interest at all.

The grantee cannot sue the grantor for defects in title, even if the grantor did not actually own the property.

Example: O executes a quitclaim deed conveying Blackacre to A. If it turns out that O did not actually own Blackacre, A has no recourse against O because a quitclaim deed carries no warranties.

권리 포기 증서(quitclaim deed)는 양수인에게 가장 적은 보호를 제공한다. 양도인은 소유권의 상태에 대해 어떠한 약정도 하지 않는다. 양수인은 양도인이 양도 시점에 가지고 있는 권리만을 양수받는 것이며, 이는 유효하지 않은 권리일 수도 있다.

양수인은 소유권의 하자에 대해 양도인에 대하여 소송을 제기할 수 없으며, 양도인이 실제로 부동산을 소유하지 않았더라도 마찬가지이다.

예시: O가 부동산을 A에게 권리 포기 증서로 양도한다. O가 실제로 부동산을 소유하지 않은 것으로 판명되면, A는 O에 대해 구제책이 없다. 권리 포기 증서에는 어떠한 보증도 없기 때문이다.

3) 특정 보증 증서(Special Warranty Deed)

The grantor warrants that there are no title defects or encumbrances that arose during the time the grantor held title, but the grantor does not warrant against defects existing before their ownership.

Example: O conveys Blackacre to A by special warranty deed. Later, a defect in title is discovered that arose before O's ownership. A cannot recover from O for this defect because a special warranty deed only covers defects during O's ownership.

특정 보증 증서(special warranty deed)에서는, 양도인이 소유권을 보유하는 동안 발생한 소유권 하자나 부담의 부존재에 대해 보증하지만, 양도인의 소유 이전에 존재하는 하자에 대해서는 보증하지 않는다.

예시: O가 부동산을 A에게 특정 보증 증서로 양도한다. 나중에 O의 소유 이전에 발생한 소유권에 대한 하자가 발견된다. A는 이 하자에 대해 O로부터 회복할 수 없다. 특정 보증 증서는 O의 소유 기간 동안의 하자만을 포함하기 때문이다.

E 부속물(Fixtures)

A fixture is tangible personal property that has been attached to real property in such a way that it is treated as part of the real property.

부속물(fixture)은 부동산에 부착되어 그 부동산의 일부로 취급되는 유형의 동산을 말한다.

1. 구조물과 자재(Structures and Materials)

Structures built on real property (e.g., walls, buildings, dams) and materials incorporated into a structure (e.g., bricks used to build a house) become part of the real property. The owner of the real property also becomes the owner of the fixture, including any materials used in constructing that structure. Once incorporated into the structure, these materials cannot be separately sold or used as collateral.

Example: O constructs a barn on Blackacre using timber. Once the barn is built, the timber is no longer personal property and becomes a fixture that is part of the real property.

부동산 위에 건설된 구조물(예: 벽, 건물, 댐)과 구조물에 통합된 자재(예: 집을 짓는 데 사용된 벽돌)는 부동산의 일부가 된다. 부동산 소유자는 해당 구조물을 건설하는 데 사용된 모든 자재를 포함하여 부속물의 소유자가 된다. 일단 구조물에 통합되면, 이러한 자재는 별도로 매도되거나 담보로 사용할 수 없다.

예시: O는 부동산에 목재를 사용하여 헛간을 건설한다. 헛간이 완성되면, 그 목재는 더 이상 동산이 아니며 부동산의 일부인 부속물이 된다.

2. 부속물의 제거(Removal of Fixtures)

The right to remove fixtures depends on who owns the real property of it.

1) Fee Simple Owner

A fee simple owner who attaches a fixture generally cannot remove the fixture unless specifically reserved in a contract of sale.

Example: Seller attaches a custom chandelier to the living room ceiling. If the seller does not expressly reserve the right to remove the chandelier in the sale agreement, the chandelier passes with the property to the buyer.

2) Tenants and Non-Freehold Possessors

A tenant or life tenant can remove fixtures that they attached, but only if (1) the property can be restored to its original condition and (2) the removal and restoration are completed within a reasonable time (typically before the lease terminates).

Example: Tenant installs a bookshelf attached to the walls of the rented apartment. If the tenant removes the bookshelf and restores the walls before vacating, they may take the bookshelf with them.

부속물을 제거할 권리는 누가 부동산을 소유하는지에 따라 달라진다.

1) 단순 소유권자(Fee Simple Owner)

부속물을 부착한 단순 소유권자는 매매계약에서 이를 명시적으로 보유하기로 약정하지 않는 한, 일반적으로 부속물을 제거할 수 없다.

예시: 매도인이 거실 천장에 맞춤형 샹들리에를 설치한다. 매도인이 매매계약에서 샹들리에를 제거할 권리를 명시적으로 보유하지 않는다면, 샹들리에는 부동산과 함께 매수인에게 이전된다.

2) 임차인 및 비자유보유 점유권자 (Tenants and Non-Freehold Possessors)

임차인이나 종신소유권자(life tenant)는 자신이 부착한 부속물을 제거할 수 있지만, 다음의 조건을 모두 충족해야 한다. 즉, (1) 부동산을 원래 상태로 복구할 수 있어야 하며 (2) 제거 및 복구가 합리적인 시간 내에 완료되어야 한다(일반적으로 임대차 종료 이전).

예시: 임차인이 임대 아파트의 벽에 부착된 책장을 설치한다. 임차인이 퇴거하기 전에 책장을 제거하고 벽을 원래 상태로 복구하면, 임차인은 그 책장을 가지고 갈 수 있다.

MEMO

V | 저당권(MORTGAGES)

A mortgage is a legal instrument that provides a lender with an interest in real property as security for the repayment of a loan or obligation. The individual who borrows funds and provides the mortgage is called the mortgagor, while the lender who receives the security interest is called the mortgagee. In most cases, the mortgagee is a bank or other financial institution.

저당권은 대출이나 채무의 상환을 담보하기 위한 담보로서 채권자에게 부동산에 대한 권리를 제공하는 법적 문서이다. 자금을 빌리고 저당권을 제공하는 개인을 저당권설정자(mortgagor)라고 하며, 담보 권리를 받는 채권자를 저당권자(mortgagee)라고 한다. 대부분의 경우, 저당권자는 은행이나 기타 금융 기관이다.

A 담보권 이론 및 소유권 이론(Lien Theory and Title Theory)

1. 담보권 이론(Lien Theory)

The mortgagor (borrower) is considered the legal owner of the property. The mortgagee (lender) only holds a lien on the property, which means the lender has a security interest but not actual title.

Example: Jack and Jill own Blackacre as joint tenants. Jack takes out a mortgage on his interest in Blackacre in a lien theory state. The mortgage does not sever the joint tenancy, and Jill will gain full title upon Jack's death.

저당권설정자(채무자)는 부동산의 법적 소유자로 간주된다. 저당권자(채권자)는 부동산에 대한 담보권만을 보유하며, 이는 저당권자가 실제 소유권이 아닌 담보권만을 가진다는 것을 의미한다.

예시: 잭과 질은 토지를 소유한다. 잭이 담보권 이론을 채택하고 있는 주에서 토지에 대한 자신의 지분에 대해 저당권을 설정한다. 저당권은 공동 연대 소유권을 단절시키지 않으며, 잭이 사망하면 질은 완전한 소유권을 얻는다.

2. 소유권 이론(Title Theory)

The mortgagor conveys legal title to the mortgagee while retaining equitable title and possession. The mortgagee holds legal title until the loan is fully repaid, at which point legal title reverts to the borrower.

Example: If Jack and Jill own Blackacre as joint tenants in a title theory state, and Jack takes out a mortgage on his share, the mortgage severs the joint tenancy. Jack and Jill will now hold Blackacre as tenants in common.

저당권설정자는 법적 소유권을 저당권자에게 이전하면서 형평법상의 소유권과 점유를 유지한다. 저당권자는 대출이 완전히 상환될 때까지 법적 소유권을 보유하며, 완전히 상환되는 시점에 법적 소유권은 채무자에게 반환된다.

예시: 잭과 질이 소유권 이론 주에서 토지를 공동 연대 소유권자로 소유하고 있으며, 잭이 자신의 지분에 대해 저당권을 설정하는 경우, 저당권은 이 공동 연대 소유권을 분리시킨다. 따라서 잭과 질은 토지를 공동 지분 소유권으로 보유하게 된다.

B 저당권 대체(Mortgage Alternatives)

Mortgage alternatives are legal mechanisms that function similarly to traditional mortgages but may offer distinct benefits or address different financial or transactional needs. Each alternative comes with its own set of rules and implications, particularly in cases of borrower default.

저당권 대체는 전통적인 저당권과 유사하게 기능하지만, 독특한 이점을 제공하거나 다른 재정적 또는 거래상의 필요를 충족시키는 법적 메커니즘이다. 각 저당권 대체는 자체의 규칙과 함의가 있으며, 특히 채무자의 채무불이행 시에 그렇다.

1. 신탁 증서(Deed of Trust)

In some states, a deed of trust is used in place of a mortgage. The borrower transfers the property title to a trustee, who holds the property in trust for the lender until the borrower repays the loan. If the borrower defaults, the lender instructs the trustee to initiate a foreclosure sale without going through judicial foreclosure proceedings.

Example: John borrows $200,000 from ABC Bank to purchase a house. Instead of a traditional mortgage, John signs a deed of trust, transferring the property to the trustee (an attorney for ABC Bank). If John defaults, the trustee can sell the property at auction to pay off the loan.

일부 주에서는 저당권 대신으로 신탁 증서(deed of trust)가 사용된다. 채무자는 부동산의 소유권을 수탁자(trustee)에게 이전하며, 수탁자는 채무자가 대출을 상환할 때까지 부동산을 채권자를 위한 신탁으로 보유한다. 채무자가 채무를 불이행하면, 채권자는 수탁자에게 사법적 담보권 실행 절차를 거치지 않고 사적 담보권 실행 경매를 시작하도록 지시한다.

예시: 존은 집을 매수하기 위해 ABC 은행으로부터 $200,000를 빌린다. 전통적인 저당권 대신, 존은 신탁 증서에 서명하여 부동산을 수탁자(ABC 은행의 변호사)에게 이전한다. 존이 채무를 불이행하면, 수탁자는 경매에서 부동산을 매각하여 대출금을 상환할 수 있다.

2. 할부 토지 계약(Installment Land Contract)

An installment land contract (also known as a contract for deed) is a financing arrangement in which (1) the seller retains legal title to the property while the buyer takes possession and agrees to make regular payments and (2) the buyer receives equitable title and gains legal title only after making the final payment.

If the buyer defaults, the seller traditionally could retain all payments and repossess the property. Modern statutes may provide protections to the buyer, treating the installment land contract similarly to a mortgage, thus requiring foreclosure or restitution to the buyer.

Example: Sarah agrees to purchase Greenacre from Tom for $150,000 through monthly installments over 10 years. Tom retains the title until Sarah makes the final payment. If Sarah defaults in the 9th year, Tom might repossess the property, but in some states, he must refund part of Sarah's payments.

Buyer Protections: States may require a seller to foreclose rather than automatically repossess the property, or may provide the buyer with an equitable right of redemption (the right to pay off the debt and regain possession).

할부 토지 계약(installment land contract)은 금융 약정이다. 즉, (1) 매도인이 법적 소유권을 유지하면서 매수인은 점유를 취득하고 정기적인 지불을 약속하며 (2) 매수인은 형평법상의 소유권을 취득하고, 최종 지불 후에만 법적 소유권을 얻는다.

매수인이 채무를 불이행하면, 전통적으로 매도인은 모든 지불금을 보유하면서 부동산을 회수할 수 있었다. 현대의 법률은 매수인에게 보호를 제공하여, 할부 토지 계약을 저당권과 유사하게 취급하고, 따라서 담보권 실행이나 매수인에 대한 보상을 요구할 수 있다.

예시: 사라는 톰으로부터 토지를 10년 동안 월별 할부로 $150,000에 매수하기로 합의한다. 톰은 사라가 최종 지불을 할 때까지 소유권을 보유한다. 사라가 9년 차에 채무를 불이행하면, 톰은 부동산을 회수할 수 있지만, 일부 주에서는 사라의 지불금 일부를 환불해야 할 수 있다.

매수인 보호(Buyer Protections): 일부 주에서는 매도인이 자동으로 부동산을 회수하는 대신 담보권 실행을 해야 하거나, 매수인에게 형평법상의 상환 권리(부채를 갚고 점유를 회복할 권리)를 제공해야 할 수 있다.

3. 절대 증서(Absolute Deed)

An absolute deed (equitable mortgage) is a deed that appears to transfer full ownership rights to the grantee. However, if the deed is given as security for a loan rather than an outright sale, it may be considered an equitable mortgage.

The borrower (grantor) transfers a deed to the lender (grantee) with the understanding that the transfer is security for a loan. If the grantor can establish that the deed was not intended to be an outright transfer but a disguised mortgage, the court will treat it as such.

Evidentiary Issues: To prove that the transaction was a disguised mortgage, the grantor must provide clear and convincing evidence. Parol evidence (oral agreements or outside evidence) is admissible to show that the absolute deed was actually intended as a security interest.

Example: John is in financial trouble and transfers his property to Alex through a deed labeled "absolute." If John can prove that the deed was actually given as collateral for a $50,000 loan, the court will treat it as a mortgage, and Alex cannot claim outright ownership.

Impact on Bona Fide Purchasers: If the grantee sells the property to a bona fide purchaser (someone who buys without notice of the underlying agreement), the original grantor cannot recover the property but may recover the value difference.

절대 증서(absolute deed)는 양수인에게 완전한 소유권을 이전하는 것으로 보이는 증서이다. 그러나 증서가 단순한 매도가 아니라 대출에 대한 담보로 제공된 경우, 이는 형평법상의 저당권(equitable mortgage)으로 간주될 수 있다.

채무자(양도인)는 채권자(양수인)에게 증서를 이전하며, 이는 대출에 대한 담보로 이해된다. 양도인이 증서가 단순한 이전이 아니라 위장된 저당권임을 입증할 수 있다면, 법원은 이를 저당권으로 취급할 것이다.

증거 문제(Evidentiary Issues): 거래가 위장된 저당권이었음을 입증하기 위해, 양도인은 명확하고 설득력 있는 증거(clear and convincing evidence)를 제공해야 한다. 구두 증거(parol evidence)는 절대 증서가 실제로 담보 권리로 의도되었음을 보여주기 위해 허용된다

예시: 존은 재정적 어려움에 처해 있으며, "절대"라고 표시된 증서를 통해 자신의 부동산을 알렉스에게 이전한다. 존이 그 증서가 실제로 $50,000 대출에 대한 담보로 제공되었음을 증명할 수 있다면, 법원은 이를 저당권으로 취급하며, 알렉스는 완전한 소유권을 주장할 수 없다.

선의의 매수인에 대한 영향(Impact on Bona Fide Purchasers): 만약 양수인이 부동산을 선의의 매수인(기초가 된 합의에 대한 통지를 받지 못하고 매수한 자)에게 매도한 경우, 원 양도인은 부동산을 회복할 수 없지만, 가치의 차이를 회복할 수는 있다.

C 저당권설정자의 양도(Transfer by Mortgagor)

When a mortgagor transfers ownership of mortgaged property to a third party, it impacts both the mortgagor's and the transferee's obligations. The rights and liabilities depend on whether the transferee assumes the mortgage obligation or takes the property subject to the mortgage.

저당권설정자가 저당 잡힌 부동산의 소유권을 제3자에게 양도하면, 저당권설정자와 양수인의 의무에 영향을 미친다. 권리와 책임은 양수인이 저당권에 대한 의무를 인수하는지 또는 저당권을 부담하는 상태로 부동산을 인수하는지에 따라 달라진다.

1. 저당권자설정자의 책임(Mortgagor's Liability)

The original mortgagor-borrower remains personally liable on the mortgage loan unless the lender agrees to release the mortgagor from liability. This means that even after transferring the property, the original borrower could still be held responsible for paying the loan if the transferee defaults.

If the transferee assumes the mortgage, the transferee becomes primarily liable, and the mortgagor becomes secondarily liable as a surety. If the transferee takes the property "subject to" the mortgage, the mortgagor remains the sole party liable for the loan.

Example: O owns Blackacre, which is subject to a $300,000 mortgage. O sells Blackacre to A, who agrees to assume the mortgage. A defaults and the property is sold at foreclosure for only $250,000. The lender can hold A liable for the $50,000 deficiency. O, as the original mortgagor, is also secondarily liable as a surety.

Example: Same facts as above, but A takes Blackacre subject to the mortgage. If A defaults, the lender can foreclose and sell Blackacre, but cannot pursue A for the deficiency. Instead, O remains liable for the remaining $50,000 debt.

Due-on-Sale Clause: A due-on-sale clause is a common mortgage provision that allows the lender to demand immediate payment of the entire loan if the property is sold or transferred without the lender's consent.

Example: T owns Greenacre and mortgages it to Lender X. T sells Greenacre to B without notifying Lender X. Because the mortgage contains a due-on-sale clause, Lender X can accelerate the mortgage and demand immediate repayment of the entire loan.

Due-on-Encumbrance Clause: A due-on-encumbrance clause permits the lender to accelerate the mortgage if the mortgagor encumbers the property with a second mortgage or additional lien.

원 저당권설정자-채무자는 채권자가 저당권설정자를 책임으로부터 면제하기로 동의하지 않는 한, 저당 대출에 대해 개인적으로 책임을 유지한다. 이는 부동산을 이전한 후에도, 양수인이 채무를 불이행하면 원 채무자가 대출금을 상환할 책임을 여전히 질 수 있음을 의미한다.

양수인이 저당권을 인수(assume)하면, 양수인은 주된 책임을 지고, 저당권설정자는 보증인(surety)으로서 2차적인 책임을 진다. 양수인이 저당권을 "부담하는(subject to)" 상태로 부동산을 취득하면, 저당권설정자는 대출에 대한 유일한 책임 당사자로 남는다.

예시: O는 $300,000의 저당권이 설정된 토지를 소유한다. O는 토지를 A에게 매도하며, A는 저당권을 인수하기로 동의한다. A가 채무를 불이행하고, 토지가 담보권 실행으로 $250,000에 매각된다. 채권자는 $50,000의 부족분에 대해 A에게 책임을 물을 수 있다. O는 원 저당권설정자로서 보증인으로서의 2차적 책임을 진다.

예시: 위의 예시와 동일한 상황이지만, A는 토지를 저당권을 "부담하는" 상태로 취득한다. A가 채무를 불이행하면, 채권자는 담보권 실행을 하고 토지를 매각할 수 있지만, A에게 부족분에 대해 추구할 수 없다. 대신, O는 남은 $50,000의 부채에 대해 책임을 진다.

매도 시 만기 조항 (Due-on-Sale Clause): 매도 시 만기 조항은 부동산이 채권자의 동의 없이 매도되거나 양도되는 경우 채무자는 기한의 이익을 상실하여 채권자가 전체 대출금을 즉시 상환하도록 요구할 수 있게 하는 일반적인 저당권 조항이다.

예시: T는 토지를 소유하고, 채권자 X에게 저당권을 설정한다. T는 채권자 X에게 알리지 않고 토지를 B에게 매도한다. 저당권에 매도 시 만기 조항이 포함되어 있으므로, 채권자 X는 전체 대출금의 즉시 상환을 요구할 수 있다.

담보 시 만기 조항 (Due-on-Encumbrance Clause): 담보 시 만기 조항은 저당권자가 부동산에 2차 저당권이나 추가 담보를 설정하는 경우 채무자는 기한의 이익을 상실하게 되는 것이다.

2. 양수인의 책임(Transferee's Liability)

The transferee-buyer may either assume the mortgage or take the property subject to the mortgage. The key difference lies in the personal liability for the mortgage debt.

1) Assuming Mortgage Obligation - Personal Liability

If the transferee assumes the mortgage, they agree to take on personal responsibility for the loan. Upon default, the transferee and the original mortgagor (now a surety) can both be held liable.

Example: Buyer X agrees to assume Seller Y's mortgage debt of $100,000. If X defaults, the lender can sue X for the full amount and hold Y liable as a surety.

2) "Subject to" Mortgage Obligation - No Personal Liability

If the transferee takes the property subject to the mortgage, they are not personally liable for the debt. The mortgagor remains the only party liable for a deficiency after foreclosure.

If the deed is silent or ambiguous regarding the transferee's liability, courts generally presume that the property was taken subject to the mortgage.

Example: A owns Whiteacre, which is subject to a $200,000 mortgage. B purchases Whiteacre from A, taking it subject to the mortgage. If B defaults, the lender can foreclose on Whiteacre but cannot seek a deficiency judgment against B. Instead, A remains liable for the remaining debt.

양수인-매수인은 저당권을 인수하거나 저당권을 부담하는(subject to) 상태로 부동산을 인수할 수 있다. 핵심적인 차이는 저당 대출에 대한 개인적 책임에 있다.

1) 저당 의무 인수(Assuming Mortgage Obligation)

양수인이 저당권을 인수하면, 대출에 대한 개인적 책임을 지는 데 동의하는 것이다. 채무불이행 시, 양수인과 원 저당권설정자가 보증인으로서 책임을 질 수 있다.

예시: 매수인 X는 매도인 Y의 $100,000 저당 부채를 인수하기로 동의한다. X가 채무를 불이행하면, 채권자는 X에게 전체 금액에 대해 소송을 제기할 수 있으며, Y는 보증인으로서 책임을 지게 된다.

2) 저당 의무 부담("Subject to" Mortgage Obligation)

양수인이 부동산을 저당권을 "부담하는" 상태로 취득하면, 부채에 대해 개인적 책임을 지지 않는다. 저당권설정자는 담보권 실행 후의 부족분에 대해 유일한 책임 당사자로 남는다.

증서에 양수인의 책임에 대한 언급이 없거나 모호한 경우, 법원은 일반적으로 부동산이 저당권을 "부담하는" 상태로 양도되었다고 추정한다.

예시: A는 $200,000의 저당권이 설정된 토지를 소유한다. B는 A로부터 토지를 매수하여 저당권을 "부담하는" 상태로 양수한다. B가 채무를 불이행하면, 채권자는 토지에 대해 담보권 실행을 할 수 있지만, B에게 부족분에 대한 판결을 추구할 수 없다. 대신, A가 남은 부채에 대해 책임을 진다.

D 저당권자의 양도(Transfer by Mortgagee)

The transfer is typically done through an assignment of mortgage document, which must be executed by the original mortgagee and accepted by the new mortgagee (assignee). This document transfers all rights, title, and interest in the mortgage to the new holder, including the right to foreclose, collect payments, and enforce the terms of the mortgage.

When a mortgage is transferred, the borrower's obligations remain unchanged. The borrower must now make payments and direct all communications to the new mortgagee. The original mortgagee typically notifies the borrower of the transfer, along with the name and contact information of the new holder.

저당권의 양도는 일반적으로 저당권 양도 문서(assignment of mortgage document)를 통해 이루어지며, 이는 원 저당권자가 작성하고 새로운 저당권자(양수인)가 수락해야 한다. 이 문서는 저당권의 모든 권리, 소유권, 부동산 권리를 새로운 보유자에게 양도하는 것이며, 여기에는 담보권 실행, 지불금 수취, 저당권 조건의 집행 권리가 포함된다.

저당권이 양도될때 채무자의 의무에는 변함이 없다. 채무자는 새로운 저당권자에게 채무를 지불하고 모든 의사소통을 해야 한다. 원 저당권자는 일반적으로 채무자에게 양도 사실과 새로운 저당권자의 이름 및 연락처 정보를 저당권설정자에게 통지한다.

E 저당권자의 점유권(Mortgagee's Right to Possession)

The mortgagee's right to possession of real property before foreclosure depends on which theory of title the jurisdiction follows. There are three main theories of title: lien theory, title theory, and intermediate theory. Each theory determines when and if the mortgagee (typically the lender) can take possession of the property before a foreclosure sale.

1) Lien Theory

Under the lien theory, the mortgage is considered a lien on the property, not a transfer of legal title. The mortgagor (borrower) retains legal and equitable title to the property, and the mortgagee (lender) has only a security interest. The mortgagee does not hold title and therefore cannot take possession of the property until after foreclosure is complete.

2) Title Theory

Under the title theory, the mortgage operates as a transfer of legal title to the mortgagee, with the mortgagor retaining equitable title. The legal title remains with the mortgagee until the debt is fully satisfied, at which point title reverts back to the mortgagor.

Because the mortgagee holds legal title, they have the right to take possession of the property at any time after default, without having to wait for the foreclosure process. This means that upon default, the mortgagee can enter the property, collect rents, lease out vacant spaces, and prevent waste.

3) Intermediate Theory

The intermediate theory is a hybrid between the lien theory and title theory. Under this theory, the mortgagor holds legal title until default. Upon default, legal title automatically vests in the mortgagee. Therefore, the mortgagee's rights to possession are similar to the title theory.

Before default, the mortgagor retains both legal and equitable title and the right to possession. Once default occurs, the mortgagee gains legal title and the right to possession. In this way, the intermediate theory functions like the lien theory before default and like the title theory after default.

4) Exception: Abandonment by Mortgagor

Regardless of the theory of title followed by a jurisdiction, the mortgagee may take possession if the mortgagor abandons the property. If the property is abandoned, the mortgagee is permitted to take steps to protect and preserve the property, even if the mortgagor is still the legal owner under lien theory.

담보권 실행 이전에 부동산에 대한 저당권자의 점유권은 해당 관할권이 따르는 소유권 이론에 따라 다르다. 세 가지 주요 소유권 이론이 있다. 즉, 담보권 이론(lien theory), 소유권 이론(title theory) 및 중간 이론(intermediate theory)이다. 각 이론은 담보권 실행 경매 전에 저당권자가 부동산을 점유할 수 있는 시기와 방법을 결정한다.

1) 담보권 이론(Lien Theory)

담보권 이론 하에서는 저당권은 부동산에 대한 담보로 간주되며, 법적 소유권의 이전이 아니다. 저당권설정자(채무자)는 부동산에 대한 법적 및 형평법상의 소유권을 유지하며, 저당권자(채권자)는 담보권만을 가진다. 저당권자는 소유권을 보유하지 않으므로, 담보권 실행이 완료될 때까지 부동산을 점유할 수 없다.

2) 소유권 이론(Title Theory)

소유권 이론 하에서는 저당권이 법적 소유권을 저당권자에게 이전하는 것으로 작용하며, 저당권자는 형평법상의 소유권을 유지한다. 법적 소유권은 부채가 완전히 상환될 때까지 저당권자에게 남아 있으며, 그 시점에 소유권은 저당권자에게 반환된다.

저당권자가 법적 소유권을 보유하므로, 채무불이행 후에는 담보권 실행 과정을 기다리지 않고 언제든지 부동산을 점유할 권리가 있다. 이는 채무불이행 시, 저당권자가 부동산에 들어가고, 임대료를 수취하고, 빈 공간을 임대하고, 낭비를 방지할 수 있음을 의미한다.

3) 중간 이론(Intermediate Theory)

중간 이론은 담보권 이론과 소유권 이론의 혼합이다. 중간 이론 하에서는 저당권설정자가 채무불이행 전까지 법적 소유권을 보유한다. 채무불이행 시, 법적 소유권이 자동으로 저당권자에게 귀속된다. 따라서 저당권자의 점유권은 소유권 이론과 유사하다.

채무불이행 전에는 저당권자가 법적 및 형평법상의 소유권과 점유권을 유지한다. 채무불이행이 발생하면, 저당권자가 법적 소유권과 점유권을 얻는다. 이러한 방식으로, 중간 이론은 채무불이행 전에는 담보권 이론처럼 작동하고, 채무불이행 후에는 소유권 이론처럼 작동한다.

4) 예외: 저당권설정자의 포기(Abandonment by Mortgagor)

관할권이 따르는 소유권 이론과 관계없이, 저당권자가 부동산을 포기한 경우 저당권자는 점유할 수 있다. 부동산이 포기된 경우, 저당권자는 저당권설정자가 여전히 법적 소유자이더라도 부동산을 보호하고 보존하기 위한 조치를 취할 수 있다.

F 담보권 실행(Foreclosure)

When a mortgagor defaults on their mortgage obligation (typically by failing to make timely payments), the mortgagee has the right to foreclose on the property. Foreclosure is the process through which the mortgagee sells the mortgaged property to satisfy the debt. The foreclosure process varies depending on the jurisdiction and the specific terms of the mortgage agreement, but it generally involves several different methods, including judicial foreclosure and non-judicial foreclosure (power of sale).

저당권설정자가 저당 의무(일반적으로 정기적인 지불 불이행)를 이행하지 못하면, 저당권자는 부동산을 담보권 실행을 할 권리가 있다. 담보권 실행은 저당권자가 부동산을 매각하여 채무를 상환하는 과정이다. 담보권 실행 절차는 관할권과 저당권 계약의 특정 조건에 따라 다르지만, 일반적으로 사법적 담보권 실행과 사적 담보권 실행(강제매각권한)가 있다.

1. 사법적 담보권 실행(Judicial Foreclosure)

Judicial foreclosure is a court-supervised process in which the mortgagee files a lawsuit to obtain a court order to foreclose on the property. This method is used in all states and is required in states that follow the lien theory of mortgages.

Process:

1) Notice: The mortgagee must provide prior notice to the mortgagor of the default and the intent to foreclose. The notice must comply with both contractual terms in the mortgage and any state-specific notice requirements.
2) Filing a Lawsuit: The mortgagee initiates the foreclosure by filing a complaint in the appropriate court.

3) Court Proceedings: The court reviews the case, and if the mortgagee proves the default, the court will issue a judgment of foreclosure.

4) Public Sale: The court will order the property to be sold at a public auction, typically conducted by the sheriff or another court-appointed official.

5) Distribution of Sale Proceeds: The proceeds from the sale are used to pay off the mortgage debt, including any accrued interest and foreclosure costs. Any remaining funds go to junior lienholders or back to the mortgagor.

사법적 담보권 실행은 저당권자가 부동산에 대한 담보권 실행을 하기 위한 법원의 명령을 얻기 위해 소송을 제기하는 법원의 감독 과정이다. 이 방법은 모든 주에서 사용되며, 저당권에 대한 담보권 이론을 따르는 주에서는 필수적이다.

절차(Process):

1) 통지(Notice): 저당권자는 채무불이행과 담보권 실행의 의사를 저당권설정자에게 사전에 통지해야 한다. 통지는 저당권의 계약 조건과 주별 통지 요구 사항을 준수해야 한다.

2) 소송 제기(Filing a Lawsuit): 저당권자는 적절한 법원에 소장을 제출하여 담보권 실행을 시작한다.

3) 법원 절차(Court Proceedings): 법원은 사건을 검토하고, 저당권자가 채무불이행을 입증하면 담보권 실행 판결을 내린다.

4) 공개 매각(Public Sale): 법원은 부동산을 공개 경매에서 매각하도록 명령하며, 일반적으로 보안관(sheriff)이나 법원에서 지정한 관리자가 이를 수행한다.

5) 매각대금의 분배(Distribution of Sale Proceeds): 매각대금은 저당 부채, 발생한 이자 및 담보권 실행 비용을 상환하는 데 사용된다. 남은 자금은 후순위 담보권자나 저당권설정자에게 돌아간다.

2. 사적 담보권 실행(Non-Judicial Foreclosure)

Non-judicial foreclosure, also known as power of sale foreclosure, is a privately conducted foreclosure method that does not require court supervision. This method is only available if the mortgage or deed of trust includes a power of sale clause, authorizing the lender to sell the property upon default without court approval.

Process:

1) Notice: The mortgagee must provide the required notice of default and intent to foreclose to the mortgagor, following the specific notice period and procedural requirements in the power of sale clause and state law.
2) Sale by Trustee: In states that use deeds of trust, the trustee (a neutral third party) is responsible for conducting the sale. The trustee must follow the notice requirements and then sell the property at a public auction.
3) Auction: The property is sold to the highest bidder, often at the county courthouse or another designated public location.
4) Distribution of Proceeds: The sale proceeds are used to satisfy the mortgage debt, with any excess funds distributed to junior lienholders and the mortgagor.

사적 담보권 실행은 법원의 감독이 필요 없는 사적으로 수행되는 담보권 실행 방법으로 강제매각권한으로 알려져 있다. 이 방법은 저당권이나 신탁 증서에 채무불이행 시 채권자가 법원의 승인 없이 부동산을 매각할 수 있도록 하는 강제매각권한 조항이 포함된 경우에만 가능하다.

절차(Process):

1) 통지(Notice): 저당권자는 채무불이행과 담보권 실행 의사를 저당권설정자에게 통지해야 하며, 강제매각권한 조항과 주법에서 요구하는 특정 통지 기간 및 절차를 따라야 한다.

2) 수탁자에 의한 매각(Sale by Trustee): 신탁 증서를 사용하는 주에서는 수탁자(중립 제3자)가 매각을 수행할 책임이 있다. 수탁자는 통지 요구 사항을 준수한 후 부동산을 공개 경매에서 매각해야 한다.

3) 경매(Auction): 부동산은 카운티 법원이나 지정된 공개 장소에서 최고 입찰자에게 매각된다.

4) 매각대금의 분배(Distribution of Proceeds): 매각대금은 저당 부채를 상환하는 데 사용되며, 남은 자금은 후순위 담보권자와 저당권자에게 분배된다.

3. 기한의 이익 상실(Acceleration Clause)

Many mortgage agreements contain an acceleration clause that allows the mortgagee to declare the entire loan balance immediately due upon default (e.g., missing a single payment). Once the acceleration clause is invoked, the entire mortgage balance must be paid to avoid foreclosure.

많은 저당권 계약에는 저당권설정자의 채무불이행 시(예: 한 번의 지불 누락) 전체 대출 잔액을 즉시 요구할 수 있는 기한의 이익 상실 조항이 포함되어 있다. 기한의 이익 상실 조항이 적용되면, 담보권 실행을 피하려면 저당권설정자는 전체 저당권 잔액을 저당권자에게 지불해야 한다.

4. 권리의 우선순위(Priority of Interests)

If there are multiple interests in the property being foreclosed (e.g., multiple mortgages, liens), a valid foreclosure terminates any junior interest to the one being foreclosed but does not affect senior interests. Determining the priority of these interests typically follows the “first in time, first in right” rule, but certain exceptions can alter this standard order.

담보권 실행의 대상인 부동산에 여러 권리(예: 복수의 저당권, 담보권)가 있는 경우, 유효한 담보권 실행은 담보권 실행이 되는 권리보다 후순위인 모든 권리를 종료시키지만, 선순위 권리에는 영향을 미치지 않는다. 이러한 권리의 우선순위를 결정하는 데에는 일반적으로 "선착순 원칙(first in time, first in right)"을 따르지만, 특정 예외가 이 순서를 변경할 수 있다.

1) 매수 자금 저당권 예외(Purchase-Money Mortgage Exception)

A purchase-money mortgage is a mortgage used to finance the purchase of the property. This type of mortgage has priority over all other non-purchase-money mortgages and liens, even those recorded earlier. The priority between two purchase-money mortgages is determined chronologically.

Example: If a seller provides financing for the buyer and takes back a mortgage to secure the debt (seller's purchase-money mortgage), it will have priority over a bank's mortgage issued at the same time. However, if both are considered purchase-money mortgages, priority is determined by the order of recording.

매수 자금 저당권(purchase-money mortgage)은 부동산 매수를 위한 자금을 조달하기 위해 사용되는 저당권이다. 이 유형의 저당권은 이전에 등록된 것이라도 모든 다른 비매수 자금 저당권 및 담보권보다 우선한다. 두 개의 매수 자금 저당권 간의 우선순위는 시간 순서에 따라 결정된다.

예시: 매도인이 매수인에게 자금을 제공하고 부채를 담보하기 위해 저당권(매도인의 매수 자금 저당권)을 취하는 경우, 이는 동시에 발행된 은행의 저당권보다 우선한다. 그러나 둘 다 매수 자금 저당권으로 간주되는 경우, 우선순위는 등록 순서에 따라 결정된다.

2) 종속 계약(Subordination Agreement)

The holder of a prior mortgage can agree to subordinate his interest to the holder of a subsequent mortgage. This agreement is enforceable unless the mortgage is not sufficiently described or specified.

Example: If Bank A (first mortgagee) agrees to subordinate its interest to Bank B (second mortgagee), then Bank B's mortgage gains priority over Bank A's.

선순위 저당권 보유자는 자신의 권리를 후순위 저당권 보유자에게 종속시키는 데 동의할 수 있다. 종속 계약은 저당권이 충분히 설명되거나 지정되지 않은 경우를 제외하고는 집행이 가능하다.

예시: 은행 A(1순위 저당권자)가 자신의 권리를 은행 B(2순위 저당권자)에게 종속시키는 데 동의하면, 은행 B의 저당권이 은행 A의 저당권보다 우선하게 된다.

3) 저당권 수정(Mortgage Modifications)

If a senior mortgagee modifies his mortgage to make it more burdensome on the mortgagor (e.g., by increasing the principal amount or interest rate), then the senior mortgagee's interest is subordinated to a subsequent mortgage only for the modified aspect. The original mortgage amount retains its senior position.

Example: If Bank A has a senior mortgage and later modifies it to increase the loan amount, Bank B's existing second mortgage will gain priority over the additional loan amount, but not over the original loan amount.

선순위 저당권자가 저당권을 채무자에게 더 부담스럽게 수정하는 경우(예: 원금액 또는 이자율 증가), 선순위 저당권자의 권리는 수정된 부분에 대해서는 후순위 저당권에 종속된다. 원래의 저당권 금액은 선순위 위치를 유지한다.

예시: 은행 A가 선순위 저당권을 가지고 있고, 나중에 대출 금액을 증가시키도록 수정하면, 은행 B의 기존 2순위 저당권은 추가 대출 금액에 대해 우선권을 갖게 되지만, 원래 대출 금액에 대해서는 그렇지 않다.

4) 등록법 예외(Recording Act Exception)

An unrecorded mortgage is subject to the state recording act, which protects subsequent purchasers and mortgagees who satisfy the requirements of the applicable recording statute.

Example: If Bank A lends money to O and takes a mortgage on O's property but fails to record, and then O grants a second mortgage to Bank B, which is recorded, Bank B's mortgage has priority under the state's recording statute.

등록되지 않은 저당권은 해당 주의 등록법의 적용을 받아 선의의 후속 저당권자보다 후순위에 있게 된다.

예시: 은행 A가 O에게 자금을 대출하고 O의 부동산에 대한 저당권을 취하지만, 등록하지 않은 경우, 이후에 O가 은행 B에게 2차 저당권을 부여하고 등록하면, 은행 B의 저당권은 주의 등록법에 따라 우선권을 가진다.

5. 담보권 실행의 효과(Effect of Foreclosure)

1) 저당권설정자(Mortgagor)

The mortgagor's interest in the property is eliminated once a valid foreclosure sale takes place. This means that the borrower no longer has any ownership rights to the property.

a) Statutory Right of Redemption

The statutory right of redemption allows the mortgagor to reclaim the property after the foreclosure sale by paying the foreclosure sale price (not just the unpaid mortgage balance) to the party who purchased the property at the foreclosure sale. This right exists in some states and provides an additional period of time (typically ranging from three months to two years) after the foreclosure sale during which the mortgagor can regain ownership.

Example: O, the mortgagor, defaults on a mortgage held by Bank A. At the foreclosure sale, X purchases the property. If O's state allows for a six-month statutory right of redemption, O can reclaim the property by paying X the full purchase price (plus any costs incurred by X) within six months after the sale.

b) Equitable Right of Redemption

The equitable right of redemption is a common law right that allows the mortgagor to prevent foreclosure and redeem the property before the foreclosure sale by paying the full amount of the mortgage debt plus any accrued interest and costs. This right exists in every jurisdiction and cannot be waived in the mortgage agreement.

Example: If a borrower has defaulted on a $150,000 mortgage, they can exercise their equitable right of redemption by paying $150,000 plus any accrued interest and fees before the foreclosure sale. If successful, the borrower retains the property, and the foreclosure process is stopped.

유효한 담보권 실행 경매로 부동산이 매각되면, 저당권설정자의 부동산에 대한 권리는 소멸된다. 이는 채무자가 더 이상 부동산에 대한 소유권을 가

지지 않음을 의미한다.

a) 법정 회수권(Statutory Right of Redemption)

법정 회수권은 저당권설정자가 담보권 실행 경매후에도 담보권 실행 매각 가격과 관련 비용을 부동산을 매수한 자에게 지급하고 부동산을 회수할 수 있도록 허용하는 것이다. 이 권리는 일부 주에서 인정하고 있으며, 담보권 실행 경매 후에 저당권설정자가 소유권을 회수할 수 있는 추가 기간(일반적으로 3개월에서 2년)을 제공한다.

예시: 저당권설정자 O가 은행 A가 보유한 저당권에 대해 채무를 불이행한다. 담보권 실행 경매에서 X가 부동산을 매수한다. O의 주에서 6개월의 법정 회수권이 허용되는 경우, O는 매각 후 6개월 이내에 X에게 전체 매수 가격 및 발생한 비용을 지불하여 부동산을 회수할 수 있다.

b) 형평법상 회수권(Equitable Right of Redemption)

형평법상 회수권은 저당권설정자가 전체 저당 부채와 발생한 이자 및 비용을 지불하여 담보권 실행 경매 전에 담보권 실행을 방지하고 부동산을 상환할 수 있도록 하는 일반법상의 권리이다. 이 권리는 모든 관할권에서 존재하며, 저당권 계약에서 포기할 수 없다.

예시: 채무자가 $150,000의 저당권을 채무불이행한 경우, 담보권 실행 경매 전에 $150,000와 발생한 이자 및 수수료를 지불하여 형평법상 회수권을 행사할 수 있다. 형평법상 회수권을 성공적으로 한 채무자는 부동산을 소유권을 유지하고 담보권 실행 절차는 중단된다.

2) 담보권 실행 경매의 부동산 매수인 (Purchaser of Property at a Foreclosure Sale)

The purchaser at a foreclosure sale takes the property subject to any senior interests but free and clear of junior interests that were part of the foreclosure action.

All junior mortgages and liens that were properly noticed and included in the foreclosure proceeding are extinguished by the foreclosure sale. The foreclosure sale does not affect senior interests, meaning the purchaser takes the property subject to the senior mortgages or liens.

Example: Bank B forecloses on a property, and X purchases it at the foreclosure sale. If Bank C's mortgage is junior to Bank B's mortgage and was part of the foreclosure action, Bank C's interest is extinguished. However, if Bank A's mortgage is senior to Bank B's, X takes the property subject to Bank A's mortgage.

담보권 실행 경매에서의 매수인은 모든 후순위 권리로부터 자유롭게 부동산을 취득하지만, 선순위 권리에 대해서는 선순위 권리를 부담하는 상태로 취득한다.

즉, 담보권 실행 절차에서 적절히 통지되고 담보권 실행 절차에 포함된 모든 후순위 저당권과 담보권은 담보권 실행 경매로 인해 소멸된다. 담보권 실행 경매는 선순위 권리에 영향을 미치지 않으므로, 매수인은 부동산을 선순위 저당권이나 담보권을 부담하는 상태로 취득한다.

예시: 은행 B가 부동산에 대해 담보권 실행을 하고, X가 담보권 실행 경매에서 부동산을 매수한다. 은행 C의 저당권이 은행 B의 저당권보다 후순위이고 담보권 실행 절차의 일부였던 경우, 은행 C의 권리는 소멸된다. 그러나 은행 A의 저당권이 은행 B보다 선순위인 경우, X는 은행 A의 저당권을 부담하는 상태로 부동산을 취득한다.

3) 선순위 권리자(Senior Interest Holders)

A foreclosure sale has no effect on the rights of a senior interest holder. Senior interests remain attached to the property, and the purchaser at the foreclosure sale takes the property subject to these senior interests.

담보권 실행 경매는 선순위 권리 보유자의 권리에 영향을 미치지 않는다. 선순위 권리는 부동산에 남아 있으며, 담보권 실행 경매의 매수인은 이러한 선순위 권리를 부담하는 상태로 부동산을 취득한다.

4) 후순위 권리자(Junior Interest Holders)

All junior interests are generally destroyed by the foreclosure of a senior interest. Junior interest holders must be given notice of the foreclosure proceeding and an opportunity to protect their interests.

If a junior interest holder is not made a party to the foreclosure action, their interest is not terminated, and they retain their lien on the property. The omitted party can initiate their own foreclosure proceeding.

Example: If Bank A forecloses on its senior mortgage and forgets to notify Bank B, which holds a second mortgage, Bank B's interest survives the foreclosure, and Bank B can foreclose against the new owner (purchaser) at the foreclosure sale.

담보권 실행으로 인해 후순위 권리는 일반적으로 소멸된다. 후순위 권리 보유자는 담보권 실행 절차에 대한 통지를 받고 자신의 권리를 보호할 기회를 가져야 한다.

후순위 권리 보유자가 담보권 실행 소송의 당사자가 되지 않은 경우, 그들의 권리는 소멸되지 않으며 부동산에 대한 담보권을 유지한다. 누락된 당사자는 자체적으로 담보권 실행 절차를 시작할 수 있다.

예시: 은행 A가 선순위 저당권으로 담보권 실행을 하고, 은행 B(2차 저당권 보유자)에 대한 통지를 잊어버린 경우, 은행 B의 권리는 담보권 실행으로 인해 소멸되지 않으며, 은행 B는 담보권 실행 경매에서의 새로운 소유자(매수인)에 대해 담보권 실행을 할 수 있다.

5) 변제순위조정 원칙(Doctrine of Marshalling of Assets)

The doctrine of marshalling of assets is an equitable doctrine used to protect junior lienholders when a senior mortgagee has a lien on multiple properties.

Under this doctrine, if a senior mortgagee holds liens on more than one property, a junior mortgagee can request that the court compel the senior mortgagee to foreclose on the properties in a manner that protects the junior lienholder's interest. This means that the senior mortgagee must first foreclose on properties not subject to the junior mortgage if possible, so long as it does not prejudice the senior mortgagee.

Example: If Bank A (Senior on Properties 1 and 2) wants to foreclose and Bank B (Junior on Property 1) has a junior interest in Property 1 only, Bank B can ask the court to require Bank A to foreclose first on Property 2 before turning to Property 1. This protects Bank B's interest, assuming Property 2's value is sufficient to satisfy Bank A's debt.

변제순위조정 원칙(doctrine of marshalling of assets)은 선순위 저당권자가 여러 부동산에 담보권을 가지고 있는 경우 후순위 담보권자를 보호하기 위해 사용되는 형평의 원칙이다.

이 원칙에 따라, 선순위 저당권자가 둘 이상의 부동산에 담보권을 가지고 있는 경우, 후순위 저당권자는 법원에 선순위 저당권자가 후순위 담보권자의 권리를 보호하는 방식으로 부동산에 대한 담보권 실행을 하도록 요구할 수 있다. 이는 선순위 저당권자가 자신에게 불이익이 발생하지 않고 가능하다면 후순위 저당권이 설정되지 않은 부동산에 대해 먼저 담보권 실행을 해야 한다는 것을 의미한다.

예시: 은행 A(부동산 1 및 2에 대한 선순위)가 담보권 실행을 하려고 하고, 은행 B(부동산 1에 대한 후순위)가 부동산 1에만 후순위 권리를 가지고 있

는 경우, 은행 B는 법원에 은행 A가 부동산 2에 먼저 담보권 실행을 하도록 요구할 수 있다. 이는 부동산 2의 가치가 은행 A의 부채를 충족시키기에 충분하다고 가정할 때 은행 B의 권리를 보호하는 것이다.

6. 경매대금의 분배(Distribution of Proceeds)

When a property is sold at a foreclosure sale, the proceeds are distributed according to a specific order of priority.

1) The proceeds are first used to pay the costs and expenses associated with conducting the foreclosure sale, such as attorney fees, court costs, publication costs, and other administrative expenses.
2) The second priority is the outstanding balance of the mortgage obligation that is the subject of the foreclosure, including any accrued interest, late fees, and other associated charges.
3) After satisfying the foreclosing mortgagee's obligation, the remaining proceeds are distributed to satisfy any junior mortgage or lien interests. The order of payment follows the principle of "first in time, first in right," unless a specific exception applies (e.g., purchase-money mortgages, subordination agreements).
4) If any funds remain after paying off all the above claims, the excess is given to the debtor-mortgagor (i.e., the original property owner).

부동산이 담보권 실행 경매에서 매각될 때, 경매대금은 특정 우선순위에 따라 분배된다.

1) 경매대금은 먼저 변호사 비용, 법원 비용, 공고 비용 및 기타 행정 비용과 같은 담보권 실행 경매와 관련된 비용과 경비를 상환하는 데 사용된다.
2) 두 번째 우선순위는 담보권 실행 대상인 저당권 채무의 미지급 잔액이며,

발생한 이자, 연체료 및 기타 관련 수수료를 포함한다.

3) 담보권 실행 저당권자의 채무를 충족한 후 남은 경매대금은 후순위 저당권 또는 담보권 권리를 충족시키는 데 사용된다. 지급 순서는 특정 예외(예: 매수 자금 저당권, 종속 계약)가 적용되지 않는 한 "선착순 원칙"에 따라 지급한다.

4) 위의 모든 청구를 상환한 후에도 경매대금이 남으면, 초과분은 채무자-저당권설정자(즉, 원 부동산 소유자)에게 반환된다.

7. 부족분과 잉여금(Deficiency and Surplus)

After a foreclosure sale, the distribution of sale proceeds often results in either a deficiency or a surplus, depending on whether the proceeds are sufficient to cover the mortgage obligation.

1) Deficiency

A deficiency occurs when the foreclosure sale proceeds are insufficient to fully satisfy the outstanding mortgage obligation owed by the mortgagor. In such a case, the mortgagee may seek to recover the remaining balance from the mortgagor through a deficiency judgment.

Example: The mortgagor owes $300,000 on a mortgage, but the property sells at foreclosure for only $250,000. The sale results in a $50,000 deficiency ($300,000 - $250,000). The lender can bring a deficiency action to recover the remaining $50,000 from the mortgagor's personal assets.

2) Surplus

A surplus occurs when the foreclosure sale proceeds are greater than the outstanding mortgage debt and other lien obligations on the property. After satisfying the mortgage obligation and any junior liens, the remaining funds are paid to the mortgagor.

> Example: The mortgagor owes $300,000 on a mortgage, and the property sells at foreclosure for $350,000. The sale results in a $50,000 surplus ($350,000 - $300,000). The lender receives the $300,000 mortgage balance, and the $50,000 surplus is returned to the mortgagor.

담보권 실행 경매 후, 경매대금의 분배는 종종 저당 의무를 충족시키기에 충분한지에 따라 부족분이나 잉여금을 발생시킨다.

1) 부족분(Deficiency)

부족분은 담보권 실행 경매대금이 저당권설정자가 채권자에게 지급해야 하는 미지급 저당 의무를 완전히 충족시키기에 부족한 경우에 발생한다. 이 경우, 저당권자는 부족분 판결(deficiency judgment)을 통해 저당권설정자에게 남은 잔액의 회수를 구할 수 있다.

예시: 저당권설정자가 $300,000를 채권자에게 빚지고 있지만, 부동산 담보권 실행 경매에서 $250,000에 매각되는 경우, 경매대금은 $50,000의 부족분($300,000 - $250,000)을 발생시킨다. 채권자는 부족한 $50,000을 채무자의 개인 자산에서 회수하기 위해 부족분 소송을 제기할 수 있다.

2) 잉여금(Surplus)

잉여금은 담보권 실행 경매대금이 미지급 저당 부채 및 부동산의 기타 담보 의무보다 큰 경우 발생한다. 저당 의무와 후순위 담보권을 충족한 후 남은 경매대금은 저당권설정자에게 지급된다.

예시: 저당권자가 $300,000를 채무자에게 빚지고 있고, 부동산이 담보권 실행에서 $350,000에 매각되는 경우, 매각은 $50,000의 잉여금($350,000 - $300,000)을 발생시킨다. 채권자는 $300,000의 저당권 잔액을 받고, $50,000의 잉여금은 저당권설정자에게 반환된다.

MEMO

VI | 타인의 토지에 대한 권리 (RIGHTS TO THE LAND OF ANOTHER)

Rights to the land of another generally refer to non-possessory interests that grant the holder certain rights to use or restrict the use of someone else's land. These rights do not confer full ownership but instead allow for specific, limited uses or control.

타인의 토지에 대한 권리는 소유권을 부여하지 않고, 소유자의 토지에 일정한 사용이나 제한을 허용하는 비점유 이익(non-possessory interests)을 말한다. 이러한 권리는 소유권이 아닌 특정한 사용 권리나 통제 권한을 제공한다.

A 지역권(Easements)

An easement is a legal right that allows the holder to use another person's land for a specific purpose. The land burdened by the easement is called the servient estate, while the land benefiting from the easement is the dominant estate. Easements can be created in various ways and have different types, each with specific rules and limitations.

지역권(easement)은 보유자가 특정한 목적을 위해 타인의 토지를 사용할 수 있도록 허용하는 법적 권리이다. 지역권으로 부담을 받는 토지를 승역지(servient estate)라고 하며, 지역권으로 이익을 얻는 토지를 요역지(dominant estate)라고 한다. 지역권은 다양한 방식으로 성립될 수 있으며, 각기 다른 유형이 존재하며, 각각 고유한 규칙과 제한이 있다.

1. 지역권의 유형(Types of Easements)

1) Easement Appurtenant

An easement appurtenant benefits a particular piece of land, known as the dominant estate. It attaches to the land and transfers automatically when the land is sold or transferred.

Example: A driveway easement allowing one property owner to cross over a neighboring property to reach their own property.

2) Easement in Gross

An easement in gross benefits an individual or entity, rather than a piece of land. It is personal to the holder and does not transfer with the land unless it is for a commercial purpose. There is no dominant estate - only a servient estate is involved.

Example: A utility company's right to run power lines across a property or a person's right to fish in a pond on another's property.

3) Affirmative Easement

An affirmative easement allows the holder to do something on the servient estate (e.g., cross the land, lay a pipeline, or enter for repairs).

Example: A right-of-way easement granting access to cross a neighbor's land to reach a road.

4) Negative Easement

A negative easement prevents the servient estate owner from doing something on their own land that would otherwise be legal. Typically involves restrictions on land use that benefit the dominant estate, such as blocking light, air, or water flow.

Example: A homeowner granting a negative easement to a neighbor to prevent building a structure that would block their view.

1) 부속지역권(Easement Appurtenant)

부속지역권은 요역지(dominant estate)로 알려진 특정 토지에 이익을 제공한다. 이는 토지에 부착되며, 토지가 매도되거나 양도될 때 자동으로 이전된다.

예시: 한 토지 소유자가 자신의 토지에 도달하기 위해 이웃 토지를 통과할 수 있도록 하는 진입로 지역권.

2) 대인지역권(Easement in Gross)

대인지역권은 특정 토지가 아니라 개인이나 단체에게 이익을 제공한다. 이는 보유자에게 개인적인 것이며, 상업적 목적이 아닌 한 토지와 함께 이전되지는 않는다. 요역지는 존재하지 않으며, 승역지만 존재한다.

예시: 전기 회사가 토지를 가로질러 전력선을 설치할 수 있는 지역권 또는 어떤 사람이 다른 사람의 토지에 있는 연못에서 낚시할 수 있는 지역권.

3) 적극적 지역권(Affirmative Easement)

적극적 지역권은 보유자가 승역지에서 어떤 행위를 할 수 있도록 허용하는 것이다(예: 토지를 통과하거나, 파이프라인을 설치하거나, 수리를 위해 들어가는 것).

예시: 도로에 도달하기 위해 이웃의 토지를 가로질러 갈 수 있는 통행 지역권.

4) 소극적 지역권(Negative Easement)

소극적 지역권은 승역지 소유자가 그들의 토지에서 법적으로 허용되는 어떤 행위를 하지 못하도록 한다. 일반적으로 요역지에 이익이 되는 토지 사용에 대한 제한을 포함하며, 빛, 공기, 수류 등을 차단하는 것을 포함한다.

예시: 주택 소유자가 조망을 막을 수 있는 구조물을 건축하지 못하도록 이웃에게 소극적 지역권을 부여하는 것.

2. 지역권의 성립(Creation of Easements)

Easements can be created in various ways, depending on the circumstances and the intent of the parties involved.

지역권은 상황과 당사자의 의도에 따라 다양한 방식으로 성립될 수 있다.

1) 명시적 지역권(Express Easement)

An express easement is created through an affirmative agreement between the parties, typically in writing, and complies with the Statute of Frauds.

Example: O, the owner of Greenacre, grants a written easement to A, giving A the right to cross Greenacre to reach a public road. This is an express easement created by the grant.

명시적 지역권(express easement)은 당사자 간의 명시적인 합의에 의해 성립되며, 일반적으로 서면으로 작성되고 사기방지법(statute of frauds)을 준수해야 한다.

예시: 토지의 소유주인 O가 A에게 토지를 가로질러 공공 도로에 도달할 수 있는 권리를 부여하는 서면 지역권을 허락한다. 이것은 명시적 수여에 의해 성립된 명시적 지역권이다.

2) 필요에 의한 지역권(Easement by Necessity)

An easement by necessity arises when a property is landlocked, meaning it has no access to a public road without crossing another's property. The easement allows the owner of the landlocked property (the dominant estate) to cross over the neighboring land (the servient estate) to reach a public road.

Easements by necessity are implied when (1) there is common ownership of both the servient and dominant estates at some point in the past and (2) the necessity for the easement arose when the land was severed into separate parcels. Unlike an easement by implication, there is no requirement for a prior use.

Example: B owns a large tract of land and subdivides it into two lots, selling one lot to A while retaining the other. A's lot is landlocked and can only access the public road by crossing B's retained lot. Even though no prior path existed and the deed makes no mention of an easement, A has an easement by necessity over B's lot.

필요에 의한 지역권(easement by necessity)은 토지가 육지로 둘러싸여 있어 다른 사람의 토지를 통과하지 않고는 공공 도로에 접근할 수 없는 경우 발생한다. 이 지역권은 육지로 둘러싸인 토지(요역지)의 소유자가 인접 토지(승역지)를 통과하여 공공 도로에 도달할 수 있도록 허용한다.

필요에 의한 지역권은 (1) 과거 어느 시점에 승역지와 요역지가 동일한 소유자에게 속해 있었고 (2) 토지가 분할되어 별도의 필지로 나뉠 때 지역권의 필요성이 발생한 경우 묵시적으로 성립된다. 묵시적 지역권과 달리, 이전 사용에 대한 요구사항은 없다.

예시: B는 큰 토지를 소유하고 이를 두 개의 필지로 분할하여 한 필지를 A에게 판매하고 다른 필지는 유지한다. A의 필지는 육지로 둘러싸여 있으며, B가 유지한 필지를 통과해야만 공공 도로에 접근할 수 있다. 이전에 경로가 존재하지 않았고 증서에 지역권에 대한 언급이 없더라도, A는 B의 필지에 대한 필요에 의한 지역권을 가진다.

3) 묵시적 지역권(Easement by Implication)

An easement by implication (also called a quasi-easement) arises when a prior use of the property existed before it was divided, and the use is reasonably necessary for the enjoyment of the dominant estate.

There must have been a prior use of the servient estate for the benefit of the dominant estate before the land was divided. The use must have been continuous and apparent at the time of severance. The easement must be reasonably necessary to the dominant estate's use and enjoyment (not strictly necessary, like in an easement by necessity).

Example: O owns a large parcel of land with a private road running through it, which O regularly uses to access a barn on the back half of the property. O sells the front half to A, which includes the beginning of the private road, but retains the back half where the barn is located. Even though no express easement is created, O has an easement by implication to continue using the private road to reach the barn.

묵시적 지역권(easement by implication)은 토지가 분할되기 전에 부동산의 이전 사용이 존재했고, 그 사용이 요역지의 이용에 합리적으로 필요할 때 발생한다.

토지가 분할되기 전에 요역지의 이익을 위해 승역지의 이전 사용이 있어야 한다. 사용은 분할 시점에 지속적이고 명백해야 한다. 지역권은 요역지의 이용과 향유에 합리적으로 필요해야 한다(필요에 의한 지역권처럼 절대적으로 필요하지는 않다).

예시: O는 사유 도로가 통과하는 큰 토지를 소유하고 있으며, O는 이를 정기적으로 사용하여 부동산의 후면에 있는 헛간에 접근한다. O는 전면부를 A에게 판매하며, 여기에는 사유 도로의 시작 부분이 포함되며, 헛간이 있는 후면부는 유지한다. 명시적 지역권이 성립되지 않았더라도, O는 헛간에 도달하기 위해 사유 도로를 계속 사용할 수 있는 묵시적 지역권을 가진다.

4) 취득시효에 의한 지역권(Easement by prescription)

An easement by prescription is similar to adverse possession but applies to use rights instead of ownership. There must be continuous, actual, open, and hostile use for a specific period but, unlike with adverse possession, the use need not be exclusive.

Example: A regularly crosses B's land to access a nearby lake for 15 years. A's use is open, without B's permission, and continuous for the statutory period. A may acquire a prescriptive easement to continue using the path to the lake.

취득시효에 의한 지역권(easement by prescription)은 소유권이 아닌 사용권에 적용된다는 점을 제외하면, 점유취득시효(adverse possession)의 요건과 유사하다. 특정 기간 동안 연속적이고 실제적이며 공개적이고 적대적인 사용이 있어야 하지만, 점유취득시효와 달리 사용이 배타적일 필요는 없다.

예시: A는 15년 동안 정기적으로 B의 토지를 가로질러 인근 호수에 접근한다. A의 사용은 공개적이고, B의 허락 없이 법정 기간 동안 지속되었다. A는 호수로 가는 경로를 계속 사용할 수 있는 취득시효에 의한 지역권을 획득할 수 있다.

5) 금반언에 의한 지역권(Easement by Estoppel)

An easement by estoppel arises when a property owner grants permission to another to use the property, and the user relies on that permission to their detriment (e.g., by making improvements or incurring expenses). The property owner may be estopped from revoking the permission if it would result in unfairness or unjust enrichment.

Example: A allows B to use a road on A's land to access B's land. B builds a home and driveway based on this access and spends substantial money improving the road. Later, A attempts to revoke permission. B may have an easement by estoppel because B reasonably relied on A's permission when making significant investments.

금반언에 의한 지역권(easement by estoppel)은 토지 소유자가 다른 사람에게 토지를 사용할 수 있는 허락을 주었고, 사용자가 그 허락에 의존하여 자신에게 불이익이 발생하는 경우(예: 개발을 하거나 비용을 지출함) 발생한다. 토지 소유자는 허락을 철회함으로써 부당함이나 부당한 이득이 발생할 경우, 허락을 철회하는 것이 금지될 수 있다.

예시: A는 B가 자신의 토지에 있는 도로를 사용하여 B의 토지에 접근할 수 있도록 허락한다. B는 이 접근을 기반으로 집과 진입로를 건설하고 도로를 개발하는 데 상당한 돈을 지출한다. 이후 A가 허락을 철회하려고 시도한다. B는 A의 허락에 합리적으로 의존하여 상당한 투자를 했으므로, 금반언에 의한 지역권을 가질 수 있다.

3. 지역권의 범위(Scope of Easement)

The scope of an easement determines the permissible uses and extent of rights granted by the easement holder. It is influenced by the nature of the easement and the original intent of the parties when the easement was created.

1) Express Easement

The scope of an express easement is defined by its express terms as stated in the deed or written agreement. If the language is ambiguous, courts will consider the parties' intent.

2) Easement by Necessity

The scope of an easement by necessity is determined strictly by the extent of the necessity that justifies its creation. It does not permit any use beyond what is absolutely necessary for the enjoyment of the dominant estate.

3) Easement by Implication

The scope of an easement by implication is determined by the nature of the quasi-easement that existed prior to the severance of the property. Changes to the scope are permissible only to the extent that they are reasonably foreseeable based on the original use.

Example: A landowner used a path on his property to access a barn, and after selling part of the property, the path becomes an easement by implication. The easement's scope is limited to uses consistent with barn access and cannot be used for unrelated purposes.

4) Easement by Prescription

The scope of an easement by prescription is limited to the nature and extent of the adverse use that created the easement.

Example: A neighbor walks through a lot to access a park for 15 years, creating a prescriptive easement. Expanding the easement for vehicle use or allowing others to use it would likely exceed the scope of the prescriptive easement.

5) Changes in the Scope of Easements

Changes in the scope are analyzed under a reasonableness standard in light of the original purpose of the easement.

No Unilateral Expansion: The owner of the dominant estate (the property benefiting from the easement) may not unilaterally expand the easement to serve a non-dominant parcel.

Example: An easement for driveway access to Lot A cannot be used to access Lot B, which the owner of Lot A purchased later, as it would constitute an impermissible expansion of the easement.

지역권의 범위는 지역권 보유자에게 부여된 권리의 허용되는 사용과 그 권리의 범위를 결정한다. 이는 지역권의 성격과 지역권이 성립될 때 당사자들의 원래 의도에 영향을 받는다.

1) 명시적 지역권(Express Easement)

명시적 지역권의 범위는 증서나 서면 계약서에 명시된 명시적 조건에 의해 정의된다. 언어가 모호한 경우, 법원은 당사자들의 의도를 고려할 것이다.

2) 필요에 의한 지역권(Easement by Necessity)

필요에 의한 지역권의 범위는 그 성립이 정당화되는 필요성의 정도에 의해 엄격히 결정된다. 이는 요역지의 향유를 위해 절대적으로 필요한 범위를 넘어서는 사용을 허용하지 않는다.

3) 묵시적 지역권(Easement by Implication)

묵시적 지역권의 범위는 토지가 분리되기 전에 존재했던 준지역권(quasi-easement)의 성격에 의해 결정된다. 범위의 변경은 원래의 사용에 기반하여 합리적으로 예견될 수 있는 범위 내에서만 허용된다.

예시: 토지 소유자가 자신의 토지에 있는 경로를 사용하여 헛간에 접근하였고, 부동산의 일부를 판매한 후 그 경로가 묵시적 지역권이 되었다면, 지역권의 범위는 헛간 접근과 일치하는 사용으로 제한되며, 관련 없는 목적으로 사용할 수 없다.

4) 취득시효에 의한 지역권(Easement by Prescription)

취득시효에 의한 지역권의 범위는 지역권을 성립한 적대적 사용의 성격과 정도로 제한된다.

예시: 이웃이 15년 동안 공원에 접근하기 위해 대지를 가로질러 걸어 다니며 취득시효에 의한 지역권을 성립하였다면, 차량 사용으로 지역권을 확장하거나 다른 사람이 사용하도록 허용하는 것은 취득시효에 의한 지역권의 범위를 넘어설 수 있다.

5) 지역권 범위의 변경(Changes in the Scope of Easements)

지역권 범위의 변경은 지역권의 원래 목적을 고려하여 합리성 기준(reasonableness standard) 하에 분석된다.

일방적 확대 불가(No Unilateral Expansion): 요역지 소유자는 비요역지(non-dominant parcel)를 위해 지역권을 일방적으로 확대할 수 없다.

예시: 부지 A에 대한 진입로 접근을 위한 지역권은 부지 A 소유자가 나중에 매수한 부지 B에 접근하기 위해 사용할 수 없으며, 이는 지역권의 허용되지 않는 확대에 해당한다.

4. 지역권의 종료(Termination of Easements)

Easements can be terminated in several ways beyond their express terms in the original agreement.

지역권은 원래의 합의에서 명시된 조건 외에도 여러 가지 방법으로 종료될 수 있다.

1) 서면포기(Release)

An easement can be terminated through an express written release by the easement holder. The release must comply with the Statute of Frauds, meaning it must be in writing and signed by the holder of the easement.

Example: A owns an easement for access across B's property. A signs a written document stating, "I hereby release my right to the easement." This release terminates the easement.

지역권은 지역권 보유자의 명시적인 서면 포기를 통해 종료될 수 있다. 이 포기는 사기방지법(statute of frauds)을 준수해야 하며, 즉 서면으로 작성되고 지역권 보유자가 서명해야 한다.

예시: A는 B의 토지를 가로질러 접근할 수 있는 지역권을 소유하고 있다. A는 "본인은 지역권에 대한 권리를 포기한다."라는 내용의 서면 문서에 서명한다. 이 포기는 지역권을 종료시킨다.

2) 필요의 종료(End of Necessity)

An easemnt by necessity terminates when the necessity no longer exists.

필요에 의한 지역권은 그 필요성이 더 이상 존재하지 않을 때 종료된다.

3) 취득시효(Prescription)

If a trespasser uses the easement and the easement holder fails to take action for the statutory period, the easement may be extinguished through adverse possession principles.

Example: A has a right of way across B's land, but B builds a structure blocking the easement. If A does not take legal action within the statutory period, the easement may be terminated by prescription.

무단 점유자가 지역권을 사용하고 지역권 보유자가 법정 기간 동안 조치를 취하지 않으면, 취득시효의 원칙에 따라 지역권이 종료될 수 있다.

예시: A는 B의 토지를 가로질러 통행할 수 있는 권리를 가지고 있지만, B가 지역권을 차단하는 구조물을 건설한다. A가 법정 기간 내에 법적 조치를 취하지 않으면, 지역권은 취득시효에 의해 종료될 수 있다.

4) 금반언(Estoppel)

An easement holder's statements or conduct that suggests abandonment, coupled with reliance by the servient estate owner, can terminate an easement by estoppel.

Example: A tells B (the servient estate owner) that A will never use the easement again, and B then builds a permanent structure on the land. A may be estopped from asserting the easement due to B's detrimental reliance.

포기를 암시하는 진술이나 행위와 승역지 소유자의 신뢰가 결합되면, 금반언에 의해 지역권이 종료될 수 있다.

예시: A는 승역지 소유자인 B에게 더 이상 지역권을 사용하지 않을 것이라고 말하고, B는 그 토지에 영구적인 구조물을 건설한다. B의 신뢰로 인해 A는 지역권을 주장하는 것이 금지될 수 있다.

5) 분리(Severance)

An appurtenant easement (an easement tied to the land) cannot be separated from the dominant estate. Any attempt to convey the appurtenant easement separately from the land it benefits results in termination of the easement.

Example: A sells his land to B but attempts to retain the easement rights. This attempt would sever and terminate the appurtenant easement.

부속지역권은 요역지로부터 분리될 수 없다. 부속지역권을 그 이익을 받는 토지와 별도로 이전하려는 모든 시도는 지역권의 종료를 초래한다.

예시: A는 자신의 토지를 B에게 매도하지만, 지역권을 유지하려고 시도한다. 이 시도는 부속지역권을 분리하여 종료시킨다.

6) 통합(Merger)

If the same person acquires ownership of both the dominant and servient estates, the easement terminates by merger. For a merger to occur, the owner must acquire fee title to both estates (complete ownership of the property). If the owner acquires less than fee title, such as a life estate or leasehold interest, merger does not occur.

Example: A has an easement to cross B's land. A purchases B's property in fee simple, making A the owner of both the dominant and servient estates. The easement is terminated by merger.

동일한 사람이 요역지와 승역지의 소유권을 모두 획득하면, 통합에 의해 지역권이 종료된다. 통합이 발생하려면, 소유자가 두 부동산 모두에 대한 소유권(fee title)을 획득해야 한다. 소유자가 종신소유권(life estate)이나 임차권(leasehold interest)과 같이 소유권보다 적은 권리를 획득하는 경우, 통합은 발생하지 않는다.

예시: A는 B의 토지를 가로질러 갈 수 있는 지역권을 가지고 있다. A가 B의 부동산에 대한 소유권(fee simple)으로 매수하여, A는 요역지와 승역지의 소유자가 된다. 지역권은 통합에 의해 종료된다.

7) 포기(Abandonment)

An easement can be terminated if the owner demonstrates clear intent to relinquish the easement right through affirmative action. Mere statements of intent or non-use are not sufficient to terminate an easement.

Example: B has a right of way across A's land but builds a permanent fence blocking the entrance to the easement. B's affirmative act of blocking the entrance is considered abandonment, terminating the easement.

소유자가 적극적인 행위를 통해 지역권 권리를 포기하려는 명확한 의도를 보이면, 지역권은 종료될 수 있다. 단순한 의도 진술이나 미사용은 지역권을 종료시키기에 충분하지 않다.

예시: B는 A의 토지를 가로질러 통행할 수 있는 권리를 가지고 있지만, 지역권의 입구를 막는 영구적인 울타리를 건설한다. 입구를 차단하는 B의 적극적인 행위는 포기로 간주되어 지역권을 종료시킨다.

B 이익권(Profit)

A profit à prendre, or simply "profit," is a specific type of easement that grants one party the right not only to enter another's land but also to remove natural resources (such as timber, minerals, oil, gas, fish, or game) from the land. In essence, it provides the holder with both the right to access the land and a right to extract something of value from the servient estate.

이익권(profit à prendre, profit)은 일정한 유형의 지역권으로, 한 당사자에게 타인의 토지에 들어갈 권리뿐만 아니라 그 토지로부터 천연자원(예: 목재, 광물, 석유, 가스, 어류, 야생동물)을 추출할 수 있는 권리를 부여한다. 본질적으로 이는 보유자에게 승역지(servient estate)에 대한 접근 권리와 그로부터 가치 있는 것을 추출할 수 있는 권리를 제공한다.

C 사용 허가(License)

A license is a non-possessory right granted to an individual to enter and use the land of another for a specific, limited purpose. Unlike more permanent interests in land, such as easements, a license is generally personal to the licensee and is freely revocable at the will of the landowner, known as the licensor, unless certain circumstances exist that make the license irrevocable.

1) No Transferability

A license is a personal privilege and is not assignable or transferable. Any attempt to transfer a license to another party generally results in its automatic termination.

2) Irrevocable Licenses

a) License Coupled with an Interest: A license coupled with an interest arises when the licensee has some other legal right to be on the land, such as the right to remove property or inspect waste.

Example: If A sells B a car and allows B to enter A's property to pick it up, B has a license coupled with an interest. This license is irrevocable until B has taken possession of the car.

b) Irrevocable License Based on Detrimental Reliance: If the licensee reasonably relies on the license and incurs expenses or makes improvements based on that reliance, the license may become irrevocable.

Example: A grants B permission to build a road across A's land to reach B's house. B spends a significant sum to build the road. A later tries to revoke the license. Because B detrimentally relied on A's permission, A may be estopped from revoking the license, creating an equitable easement.

사용 허가(license)는 특정하고 제한된 목적을 위해 타인의 토지에 들어가 사용하도록 개인에게 부여되는 비점유권(non-possessory right)이다. 지역권과 같은 영구적인 토지에 대한 권리와는 달리, 사용 허가는 일반적으로 허가받은 자(licensee)에게 개인적인 것이며, 토지 소유자인 허가자(licensor)의 의지에 따라 자유롭게 취소될 수 있다. 단, 사용 허가를 취소할 수 없게 만드는 일정한 상황이 존재하지 않는 한 그렇다.

1) 양도 불가성(No Transferability)

사용 허가는 개인적 특권이며, 양도하거나 이전할 수 없다. 사용 허가를 다른 당사자에게 이전하려는 모든 시도는 일반적으로 사용 허가를 자동으로 종료하게 된다.

2) 철회 불가능 사용 허가(Irrevocable Licenses)

a) 이익과 결합된 사용 허가(License Coupled with an Interest): 허가받은 자가 토지에 있을 수 있는 다른 법적 권리(예: 재산을 제거하거나 폐기물을 검사할 권리)를 가지고 있을 때 발생한다.

예시: A가 B에게 자동차를 판매하고, B가 이를 가져가기 위해 A의 부동산에 들어가는 것을 허락하는 경우, B는 이익과 결합된 사용 허가를 가진다. 이 사용 허가는 B가 자동차를 인도받을 때까지 취소할 수 없다.

b) 손해유발 신뢰 기반한 철회 불가능한 사용 허가(Irrevocable License Based on Detrimental Reliance): 허가받은 자가 사용 허가에 합리적으로 신뢰하고 그 신뢰에 기반하여 비용을 지출하거나 개발을 하는 경우에는 사용 허가는 취소할 수 없게 될 수 있다.

예시: A가 B에게 B의 집에 도달하기 위해 A의 토지를 가로질러 도로를 건설할 수 있는 허가를 부여한다. B는 도로를 건설하기 위해 상당한 금액을 지출한다. 이후 A가 사용 허가를 취소하려고 한다. B가 A의 허가에 대해 손해유발 신뢰를 했기 때문에, A는 사용 허가를 취소하는 것이 금지될 수 있으며, 이는 형평법상의 지역권(equitable easement)을 성립한다.

D 약정(Covenants)

Covenants are legally enforceable agreements that restrict the use of land that are intended to bind future owners and affect the property's use. There are two types of convenants - real covenants and equitable servitudes. The key distinction between them is the remedy sought: real covenants are enforced through damages, whereas equitable servitudes are enforced through injunctions.

약정(covenants)은 부동산의 사용을 제한하고 미래의 소유자들에게 구속력을 가지며 부동산의 이용에 영향을 미치는 법적으로 집행 가능한 합의이다. 약정에는 두 가지 유형이 있는데, 실제 약정(real covenants)과 형평법상 구속(equitable servitudes)이 있다. 이 둘의 주요 차이점은 구제책에 있다. 실제 약정의 구제는 손해배상인 반면, 형평법상 구속의 구제는 금지명령이다.

1. 실제 약정(Real Covenants)

1) 약정이 토지와 함께 이전되기 위한 요건 (Requirements for Covenants to Run with the Land)

For a covenant to run with the land and bind or benefit subsequent owners, several requirements must be met. These elements must be satisfied for both the burden and the benefit of the covenant to run with the land.

약정이 토지와 함께 이전되어 후속 소유자에게 구속되거나 이익이 되려면, 여러 요건을 충족해야 한다. 이러한 요건들은 약정의 부담과 이익이 모두 토지와 함께 이전되기 위해 필요하다.

a) 서면(Writing)

The covenant must be created by a written instrument that complies with the Statute of Frauds.

약정은 사기방지법(statute of frauds)을 준수하기 위해 서면으로 작성되어야 한다.

b) 의도(Intent)

The original parties must have intended for the covenant to run with the land. This intent can be demonstrated by explicit language in the covenant (e.g., "and his heirs and assigns") or can be implied from the circumstances.

원 당사자들은 약정이 토지와 함께 이전되도록 의도해야 한다. 이 의도는 약정에 명시적인 언어(예: "그의 상속인과 양수인에게")로 나타낼 수 있으며, 상황으로부터 묵시적으로 추론될 수도 있다.

c) 토지 관련성(Touch and Concern)

The covenant must "touch and concern" the land, meaning it must affect the parties as landowners rather than merely as individuals. The covenant must have an impact on the legal rights associated with owning the land. Generally, this means the covenant must relate to the use, value, or enjoyment of the land.

Examples: A covenant requiring all homeowners in a subdivision to maintain their lawns affects the enjoyment and value of the land and therefore touches and concerns the land.

약정은 토지 관련성(touch and concern)이 있어야 한다. 이는 약정이 단순히 개인으로서가 아니라 토지 소유자로서 당사자들에게 영향을 미쳐야 함을 의미한다. 약정은 토지 소유와 관련된 법적 권리에 영향을 미쳐야 한다. 일반적으로 이는 약정이 토지의 사용, 가치 또는 향유와 관련되어야 함을 의미한다.

예시: 구획 내 모든 주택 소유자들이 잔디를 유지하도록 요구하는 약정은 토지의 향유와 가치에 영향을 미치므로 토지 관련성이 있게 된다.

d) 통지(Notice - for Burden)

For the burden of a covenant to bind a subsequent purchaser, the purchaser must have notice of the covenant.

Notice can be (1) actual notice (the purchaser is personally aware of the covenant), (2) constructive notice (the covenant is recorded in the public record), or (3) inquiry notice (the condition of the property itself should have prompted the purchaser to inquire further).

Example: If a buyer is purchasing a property with visible fencing that conforms to subdivision regulations, the buyer may have inquiry notice of covenants requiring uniform fencing.

약정의 부담이 후속 소유자를 구속되기 위해서는 매수인이 약정에 대한 통지를 받아야 한다.

통지는 (1) 실제 통지(매수인이 약정에 대해 개인적으로 알고 있음) (2) 의제 통지(약정이 공적 기록에 등록되어 있음) 또는 (3) 조사 통지(부동산의 상태 자체가 매수인으로 하여금 추가 조사를 하도록 함)가 있다.

예시: 매수인이 구획 규정에 부합하는 눈에 보이는 울타리가 있는 부동산을 구매하는 경우, 매수인은 통일된 울타리를 요구하는 약정에 대한 조사 통지가 있을 수 있다.

e) 관계(Privity)

There are two types of privity that affect whether a covenant will run:

i) Horizontal Privity

Privity of estate between the original parties to the covenant at the time the covenant is created. The parties must have shared some interest in the land, such as a grantor-grantee or landlord-tenant relationship.

Horizontal privity is required only for the burden of a covenant to run.

ii) Vertical Privity

Privity of estate between the original party to the covenant and the successor in interest. The successor must hold the same estate as the original party (for the burden to run, the successor must hold the entire interest).

Vertical privity is required for both the benefit and the burden of a covenant to run.

Example: If the original party holds a fee simple and the successor holds only a life estate, vertical privity is lacking for the burden to run.

약정의 이전 여부에 영향을 미치는 두 가지 유형의 관계(privity)[7]가 있다.

7) 현대적 추세는 관계(Privity) 요건에 대한 엄격한 요구를 하지 않는 쪽으로 바뀌고 있다. Restatement (Third) of Property에서는 이 관계 요건을 요구하지 않는다. 대신 약정의 성격과 공공 정책적 고려에 초점을 맞춘다. 그 결과 약정이 토지 이용과 관련된 명확한 목적을 제공하고 부당한 부담을 부과하지 않는다면 관계는 항상 필요한 것은 아니다.

i) 수평적 관계(Horizontal Privity)

약정이 성립될 때 원 당사자들 간의 부동산에 대한 관계다. 당사자들은 양도인-양수인 또는 임대인-임차인 관계와 같이 토지에 대한 어떤 이익을 공유해야 한다.

수평적 관계는 약정의 부담이 이전되기 위해서만 필요하다.

ii) 수직적 관계(Vertical Privity)

약정의 원 당사자와 승계인 간의 부동산 권리에 대한 관계다. 승계인은 원 당사자와 동일한 부동산권을 보유해야 한다(부담이 이전되기 위해서는 승계인이 전체 이익을 보유해야 한다).

수직적 관계는 약정의 이익과 부담이 모두 이전되기 위해 필요하다.

예시: 원 당사자가 단순 소유권(fee simple)을 보유하고 승계인이 종신소유권(life estate)만을 보유하는 경우, 부담이 이전되기 위한 수직적 관계로 충분하지 않게 된다.

2) 실제 약정의 예시(Example of a Real Covenant)

Smith, subdivides a large tract of land into a new residential neighborhood called Maplewood Heights. Smith sells a lot to a buyer, John, and includes a restrictive covenant in the deed, stating, "The lot must be used only for residential purposes, and no building shall be constructed that exceeds two stories in height."

Smith then sells another lot to Emma, and her deed also contains the same restrictive covenant. The covenant is intended to run with the land, and it explicitly states that the restriction is binding on all subsequent owners and enforceable by each lot owner against all others.

Several years later, John sells his lot to a new owner, Alice, who decides to build a three-story house on her property. Emma, still living in the neighborhood, wishes to enforce the two-story height restriction against Alice because the covenant was created to maintain a uniform look and protect the value of the homes in the neighborhood.

Analysis of Real Covenant Elements:

For the burden of the real covenant to run with the land to Alice and be enforceable by Emma, the following requirements must be met:

a) Writing: The restriction was included in a written deed.
b) Intent: The original parties (Smith and John) intended for the restriction to bind successors.
c) Touch and Concern: The restriction impacts the use and enjoyment of the land.
d) Notice: Alice likely had notice of the restriction through recorded documents or because it is obvious from the nature of the neighborhood.
e) Horizontal Privity: There was horizontal privity between the original parties (Smith and John) because the covenant was created at the time of the conveyance of the estate.
f) Vertical Privity: Alice holds the same estate (fee simple) as John, the original burdened party, making her a successor in interest.

If these requirements are satisfied, Emma can bring a claim for damages against Alice for violating the real covenant. If Emma sought injunctive relief instead, the court would treat the claim as an equitable servitude, for which privity is not required.

Smith는 큰 토지를 분할하여 Maplewood Heights라는 새로운 주거 지역을 조성한다. Smith는 John에게 한 필지를 판매하면서, 증서에 다음과 같은 제한 약정을 포함시킨다. 즉 "해당 필지는 주거 목적에만 사용되어야 하며, 2층을 초과하는 건물을 건설해서는 안 된다." 라는 약정이다.

Smith는 이후 Emma에게 또 다른 필지를 매도하며, 그녀의 증서에도 동일한 제한 약정이 포함되어 있다. 약정은 토지와 함께 이전되도록 의도되었으며, 그 제한이 모든 후속 소유자에게 구속되며 각 필지 소유자가 다른 소유자들에게 집행할 수 있음을 명시적으로 언급하고 있다.

몇 년 후, John은 자신의 필지를 새로운 소유자인 Alice에게 매도하고, Alice는 자신의 부동산에 3층짜리 집을 짓기로 결정한다. 여전히 그 지역에 거주하는 Emma는 약정이 지역의 통일된 외관을 유지하고 주택의 가치를 보호하기 위해 성립되었기 때문에, Alice에게 2층 높이 제한을 집행하기를 원한다.

실제 약정 요소의 분석(Analysis of Real Covenant Elements)

실제 약정의 부담이 토지와 함께 Alice에게 이전되어 Emma에 의해 집행되기 위해서는 다음의 요건을 충족해야 한다.

a) 서면(Writing): 제한 사항은 서면 증서에 포함되었다.
b) 의도(Intent): 원 당사자들(Smith와 John)은 제한이 승계인들을 구속하기를 의도했다.
c) 토지 관련성(Touch and Concern): 제한은 토지의 사용과 향유에 영향을 미친다.
d) 통지(Notice): Alice는 등록된 문서를 통해 또는 지역의 성격으로 인해 제한에 대한 통지가 있었을 가능성이 높다.
e) 수평적 관계(Horizontal Privity): 원 당사자들(Smith와 John) 간에 수평적 관계가 있었다. 이는 약정이 부동산의 양도 시점에 성립되었기 때문이다.
f) 수직적 관계(Vertical Privity): Alice는 John과 동일한 부동산권(단순 소유권)을 보유하고 있어 승계인이 된다.

이러한 요건이 충족되면, Emma는 Alice가 실제 약정을 위반한 것에 대해 손해배상 청구를 제기할 수 있다. 만약 Emma가 손해배상 대신 금지명령 구제를 요청한다면, 법원은 그 청구를 형평법상 구속(equitable servitude)으로 취급할 것이며, 이를 위해서는 관계(privity)가 필요하지 않게 된다.

2. 형평법상 구속(Equitable Servitudes)

An equitable servitude is a restriction on the use of land that is enforced in equity rather than at law. This means that the remedy for a breach is usually injunctive relief, rather than money damages.

Requirements for an Equitable Servitude to Run with the Land:

1) Writing

The equitable servitude must be created by a written instrument that complies with the Statute of Frauds.

2) Intent

The original parties must intend for the restriction to apply to successors in interest.

3) Touch and Concern

Like real covenants, the equitable servitude must "touch and concern" the land, which means it must affect the owners as landowners, not merely as individuals. The restriction should relate to the use, value, or enjoyment of the land.

4) Notice (for Burden to Run)

The party against whom the servitude is being enforced must have notice of the restriction.

5) No Privity Requirement

Unlike real covenants, privity (either horizontal or vertical) is not required for equitable servitudes to run. This means that even successors who do not hold the same estate as the original party can be bound or benefit from the servitude.

Example: A subdivision owner sells lots with a common restriction, such as a height limit on buildings. Subsequent owners are still bound by the restriction even if they do not share privity with the original party.

형평법상 구속은 법률이 아닌 형평법에서 집행되는 토지 사용에 대한 제한이다. 이는 위반에 대한 구제책이 일반적으로 금지명령과 같은 형평법상의 구제이며, 손해배상이 아니라는 것을 의미한다.

형평법상 구속이 토지와 함께 이전되기 위한 요건(Requirements for an Equitable Servitude to Run with the Land)

1) 서면(Writing)

형평법상 구속은 사기방지법(statute of frauds)을 준수하는 서면 문서로 성립되어야 한다.

2) 의도(Intent)

원 당사자들은 제한이 승계인들에게 적용되도록 의도해야 한다.

3) 토지 관련성(Touch and Concern)

실제 약정과 마찬가지로, 형평법상 구속은 토지 관련성이 있어야 하며, 이는 약정이 단순히 개인으로서가 아니라 토지 소유자로서 소유자들에게 영향을 미쳐야 함을 의미한다. 제한은 토지의 사용, 가치 또는 향유와 관련되어야 한다.

4) 통지(부담의 이전을 위해)(Notice for Burden to Run)

형평법상 구속을 부담하는 당사자는 제한에 대한 통지를 받아야 한다.

5) 관계 미요구(No Privity Requirement)

실제 약정과 달리, 형평법상 구속이 이전되기 위해서는 수평적 관계와 수직적 관계가 필요하지 않다. 이는 원 당사자와 동일한 부동산권을 보유하지 않는 승계인들도 구속의 제한을 받거나 이익을 받을 수 있음을 의미한다.

예시: 토지 소유자가 건물의 높이 제한과 같은 공통된 제한이 있는 필지를 매도한다. 후속 소유자들은 원 당사자와 관계를 공유하지 않더라도 여전히 그 제한에 구속된다.

3. 묵시적 형평법상 구속(Implied Equitable Servitudes)

Implied equitable servitudes arise when there is a common scheme or plan for development, and the servitude applies to all lots in the scheme even without a written agreement. This is common in planned communities or subdivisions. It is also known as Implied reciprocal servitudes or Reciprocal negative servitudes

묵시적 형평법상 구속은 개발에 대한 공통 계획이나 구상이 있을 때 발생하며, 서면 합의가 없더라도 그 구속은 계획 내의 모든 토지에 적용된다. 이는 계획된 커뮤니티나 구획내에서 일반적이다. 이는 묵시적 상호 구속(implied reciprocal servitudes) 또는 상호 소극적 구속(reciprocal negative servitudes)이라고도 한다.

1) 묵시적 형평법상 구속의 요건(Elements for an Implied Equitable Servitude)

a) Intent to Create a Servitude (Common Scheme)

The original grantor (often a developer) must have intended to create a common scheme of development that includes uniform restrictions on all properties within the subdivision.

The common scheme is typically established when the subdivision was first created and is evidenced by maps, plats, or deeds that include similar restrictions.

b) Negative Servitude

The servitude must be negative, meaning it imposes a restriction on what property owners cannot do (e.g., prohibiting commercial use or requiring residential use only).

Affirmative obligations (such as maintenance) are not typically enforced as implied servitudes unless expressly stated.

c) Notice

The party against whom enforcement is sought must have notice of the servitude. Notice can be established in three ways (1) actual notice (the owner was directly informed of the restriction); (2) record notice (the restriction is recorded in the public records); or (3) inquiry notice (there are visible indications of the restriction, such as a uniform appearance of homes or landscaping, which would lead a reasonable buyer to inquire about the existence of covenants).

a) 구속을 성립시키려는 의도(Intent to Create a Servitude)

원 양도인(종종 개발자)은 구획 내의 모든 부동산에 대한 통일된 제한을 포함하는 공통된 개발 계획을 성립시키려는 의도가 있어야 한다.

공통 계획은 일반적으로 구획이 처음 조성될 때 확립되며, 유사한 제한을 포함하는 지도, 도면 또는 증서에 의해 입증된다.

b) 소극적 구속(Negative Servitude)

구속은 소극적이어야 하며, 이는 부동산 소유자에게 제한을 가하여 어떠한 행위를 할 수 없게 하는 것을 의미한다(예: 상업적 사용 금지 또는 주거용 사용만 허용).

명시적으로 언급되지 않는 한, 유지보수 같은 적극적 의무는 일반적으로 소극적 구속으로 집행되지 않는다.

c) 통지(Notice)

집행의 대상이 되는 당사자는 구속에 대한 통지를 받아야 한다. 통지는 세 가지 방식이 될 수 있다. 즉, (1) 실제 통지(소유자가 제한에 대해 직접 통보를 받음) (2) 의제 통지(제한이 공적 기록에 등록되어 있음) (3) 조사 통지(주택이나 조경의 통일된 외관과 같은 제한의 가시적인 표시가 있어 합리적인 매수인이 약정의 존재에 대해 조사하도록 하는 경우).

2) 묵시적 형평법상 구속의 예시(Example of an Implied Equitable Servitude)

A developer creates a 50-lot residential subdivision and records a subdivision map indicating that all properties are subject to a residential-use-only restriction. The first 40 deeds include language prohibiting any commercial use of the properties, but 10 deeds do not include this restriction.

a) Intent to Create a Servitude: The recorded map, along with the majority of the deeds including the restriction, indicates an intent to create a common scheme.

b) Negative Servitude: The restriction is negative because it prohibits commercial use.

c) Notice: Subsequent purchasers of the 10 lots without express restrictions have record notice because the map is recorded, and inquiry notice because a reasonable buyer would notice that most deeds in the subdivision include the restriction.

In this case, even though 10 of the deeds do not have the residential-use-only restriction, a court may find that the implied equitable servitude applies to those lots and enjoin any commercial use.

개발자가 50개 필지의 주거용 구획을 조성하고, 모든 부동산이 주거용으로만 사용된다는 제한을 나타내는 구획 지도를 등록한다. 첫 40개의 증서에는 부동산의 상업적 사용을 금지하는 언어가 포함되어 있지만, 10개의 증서에는 이 제한이 포함되어 있지 않다.

a) 구속을 생성하려는 의도(Intent to Create a Servitude): 등록된 지도와 제한을 포함하는 대부분의 증서는 공통된 계획을 생성하려는 의도를 나타내고 있다.

b) 소극적 구속(Negative Servitude): 제한은 상업적 사용을 금지하므로 소

극적 구속에 해당한다.

c) 통지(Notice): 명시적 제한이 없는 10개 필지의 후속 매수인들은 지도가 등록되어 있으므로 의제 통지를 받았으며, 구획의 대부분의 증서에 제한이 포함되어 있다는 사실을 합리적인 매수인이 알 수 있으므로 조사 통지도 있게 된다.

이 사례에서, 비록 10개의 증서에 주거용으로만 사용된다는 제한이 없더라도, 법원은 그 필지들에 묵시적 형평법상 구속이 적용되어 상업적 사용을 금지할 수 있다고 판단할 것이다.

3) 형평법상 항변(Equitable Defense)

a) General Equitable Defenses

A defendant may raise several defenses to the enforcement of an equitable servitude, including acquiescence (the servitude holder has failed to object to similar violations by others); abandonment (the servitude has been so routinely violated that it is no longer enforceable); unclean hands (the party seeking enforcement has violated the servitude themselves); or laches (there was an unreasonable delay in enforcing the servitude, and enforcing it now would prejudice the defendant).

b) Changed Conditions Doctrine

A common defense to the enforcement of an implied equitable servitude is the changed conditions doctrine. This defense allows a property owner to argue that the restriction is no longer enforceable due to drastic changes in the surrounding area that have rendered the restriction useless or inequitable. The party seeking to terminate the restriction bears the burden of proving that the changes are so substantial that the restriction should no longer be enforced.

Minor or moderate changes are not sufficient; the entire restricted area must have changed in such a way that the restriction no longer provides any benefit to the affected properties.

Example: A small subdivision was originally developed as a residential community with a restriction limiting each lot to single-family homes only. Decades later, a major highway is built nearby, and the surrounding area has become largely commercial. If the residential character of the subdivision is destroyed and the lots are no longer suitable for single-family use, a court may find that enforcing the residential-only restriction is unreasonable and may decline to enforce it.

a) 일반적 형평법상 항변(General Equitable Defenses)

피고는 형평법상 구속의 집행에 대해 여러 가지 항변을 제기할 수 있는데, 여기에는 묵인(acquiescence) (다른 사람들의 유사한 위반에 대해 이의를 제기하지 않은 경우), 포기(abandonment) (부담이 너무 일상적으로 위반되어 더 이상 집행될 수 없는 경우), 부정한 손 원칙(unclean hands) (집행을 구하는 당사자가 스스로 부담을 위반한 경우) 또는 권리행사 태만(laches) (부담을 집행하는 데 부당한 지연이 있었고, 지금 집행하면 피고에게 불이익을 주는 경우)가 포함된다.

b) 변화된 환경의 원칙(Changed Conditions Doctrine)

묵시적 형평법상 구속의 집행에 대한 항변으로 변화된 환경의 원칙이 있다. 이 항변은 부동산 소유자가 주변 지역의 극적인 변화로 인해 제한이 무용적이거나 형평에 맞지 않게 되어 더 이상 집행될 수 없다고 주장할 수 있도록 한다. 제한을 종료하려는 당사자는 변화가 매우 커서 제한을 더 이상 집행해서는 안 된다는 것을 입증할 책임이 있다.

작거나 중간 정도의 변화는 충분하지 않으며, 제한된 전체 지역이 영향을 받는 부동산에 더 이상 어떤 이익도 제공하지 않도록 변경되어야 한다.

예시: 작은 구획이 원래 단독 주택만 허용하는 제한을 가진 주거 커뮤니티로 개발되었다. 수십 년 후, 인근에 주요 고속도로가 건설되고 주변 지역이 대부분 상업적으로 변했다. 분양지의 주거적 특성이 파괴되고 필지가 더 이상 단독 주택용으로 적합하지 않다면, 법원은 주거용으로만 사용된다는 제한을 집행하는 것이 불합리하다고 판단하여 이를 집행하지 않을 수 있다.

VII | 토지 소유권에 부수하는 권리 (RIGHTS INCIDENTAL TO LAND OWNERSHIP)

Rights incidental to land ownership are additional rights that come with possessing a piece of real property.

토지 소유권에 부수하는 권리는 부동산을 소유함에 따라 수반되는 추가적인 권리이다.

A 지지권(Support Rights)

Support rights refer to a landowner's right to have their land maintained in its natural condition without being destabilized by neighboring property activities.

지지권은 인접한 토지의 활동으로 인해 자신의 토지가 불안정해지지 않고 자연 상태로 유지될 수 있는 토지 소유자의 권리를 말한다.

1. 횡적 지지(Lateral Support)

Lateral support refers to the support a piece of land receives from the adjoining properties at its sides. If an adjoining landowner engages in excavations or other activities that result in a loss of this support, they may be held liable for damages under specific conditions.

1) Strict Liability for Natural Land

A landowner is strictly liable for any damage to adjoining land that results from excavation if the adjoining land is in its natural state (i.e., undeveloped land).

Example: Owner excavates his property, causing Neighbor's undeveloped land to collapse. Because Neighbor's land was in its natural state, Owner is strictly liable for the damage.

2) Improved Land - Strict Liability or Negligence

If the adjoining land has been improved (e.g., by building a house or other structures), strict liability applies only if the land would have collapsed in its natural state (regardless of the improvements).

If the weight of the improvements on the adjoining land contributes to the collapse, then the excavating landowner is not strictly liable. Instead, the adjoining landowner must prove that the excavation was negligent to recover damages.

Example: Owner's excavation causes Neighbor's land, along with a house on it, to subside (collapse or sink). Owner is strictly liable if the land would have subsided even without the house. However, if the house's weight contributed to the subsidence, Neighbor must prove that Owner was negligent in conducting the excavation.

횡적 지지(lateral support)는 토지가 측면에서 인접한 부동산으로부터 받는 지지를 의미한다. 인접한 토지 소유자가 굴착이나 기타 활동을 하여 이러한 지지를 상실하게 하는 경우, 특정 조건 하에서 손해에 대한 책임을 질 수 있다.

1) 자연 상태의 토지에 대한 엄격 책임(Strict Liability for Natural Land)

인접한 토지가 자연 상태(즉, 미개발된 토지)인 경우, 토지 소유자는 자신의 굴착으로 인해 인접 토지에 발생한 모든 손해에 대해 엄격 책임을 진다.

예시: 소유자가 자신의 토지를 굴착하여 이웃의 미개발된 토지가 붕괴되었다. 이웃의 토지가 자연 상태였으므로, 소유자는 그 손해에 대해 엄격 책임을 진다.

2) 개발된 토지(Improved Land) - 엄격 책임 또는 과실 책임

인접한 토지가 개발된 경우(예: 주택이나 기타 구조물이 건설된 경우), 엄격 책임은 토지가 개발과 관계 없이 자연 상태에서도 붕괴되었을 경우에만 적용된다.

인접 토지의 개발물의 무게가 붕괴에 기여한 경우, 굴착한 토지 소유자는 엄격 책임을 지지 않는다. 대신, 인접 토지 소유자는 손해 배상을 받기 위해 굴착이 과실로 이루어졌음을 입증해야 한다.

예시: 소유자의 굴착으로 인해 이웃의 토지와 그 위의 주택이 침하되었다. 주택이 없었더라도 토지가 침하되었을 경우, 소유자는 엄격 책임을 진다. 그러나 주택의 무게가 침하에 기여했다면, 이웃은 소유자가 굴착을 수행하는 데 과실이 있었음을 입증해야 한다.

2. 하층 지지(Subjacent Support)

Subjacent support refers to support from beneath the surface of the land, which becomes relevant when rights to the underground resources (e.g., mining rights) are sold separately from the surface rights.

1) Support for Land and Pre-Existing Improvements

If a landowner grants the right to mine or extract minerals beneath the surface, the grantee (e.g., the mining company) is strictly liable for damage to the surface land and any buildings or structures that existed at the time of the conveyance of the mining rights.

Example: A landowner sells mining rights to a third party. The mining activity causes the land to sink, damaging a barn that was present when the rights were sold. The mining company is strictly liable for the damage to the land and the barn.

2) Support for Later Improvements

The owner of the underground rights is liable for damage to later-constructed buildings or structures only if the owner was negligent in maintaining the support.

Example: If a homeowner builds a new garage after selling the underground rights and the mining activity later causes the garage to sink, the mining company is only liable if the homeowner can prove negligence in conducting the mining operations.

하층 지지(subjacent support)는 토지의 지표 아래로부터의 지지를 의미하며, 이는 지하 자원(예: 광업권)에 대한 권리가 지표권과 별도로 제공될 때 관련된다.

1) 토지와 기존 개발물에 대한 지지
(Support for Land and Pre-Existing Improvements)

토지 소유자가 지표 아래에서 광업이나 광물 채굴할 권리를 부여한 경우, 수취인(예: 광업 회사)은 광업권의 양도 시점에 존재했던 지표 토지 및 건물이나 구조물에 대한 손해에 대해 엄격 책임을 진다.

예시: 토지 소유자가 제3자에게 광업권을 제공한다. 광업 활동으로 인해 토지가 침하되어, 권리가 제공될 때 존재했던 헛간이 손상되었다. 광업 회사는 토지와 헛간에 대한 손해에 대해 엄격 책임을 진다.

2) 권리 제공 후 개발물에 대한 지지(Support for Later Improvements)

지하 권리의 소유자는 권리 제공 후에 건설된 건물이나 구조물에 대한 손해에 대해, 지지를 유지하는 데 과실이 있었을 경우에만 책임이 있다.

예시: 주택 소유자가 지하 권리를 제공한 후 새로운 차고를 건설했고, 이후 광업 활동으로 인해 차고가 침하되었다면, 주택 소유자가 광업 활동 수행에 과실이 있었다는 것을 입증할 경우에만 광업 회사가 책임을 진다.

B 수리권(Water Rights)

Water rights define the legal framework that determines who has access to water resources and how they may be used. The governing doctrine depends on the jurisdiction, with different rules for surface water and ground water.

수리권(water rights)은 누가 수자원에 접근할 수 있고 어떻게 사용할 수 있는지를 결정하는 법적 권리이다. 적용되는 원칙은 관할권에 따라 다르며, 지표수 및 지하수에 대한 규칙이 다르다.

1. 수리권의 이론(Theories of Water Rights)

1) Riparian Rights

The riparian doctrine states that water belongs to those who own the land bordering the water course. Riparian landowners share the right to reasonable use of the water and are not permitted to substantially interfere with other riparians' use of the water. Under the riparian system, domestic use (e.g., household use) trumps commercial use (e.g., irrigation or industry) and can be unlimited as long as it is reasonable.

Example: If a farmer diverts water from a stream bordering his property for irrigation, but this action significantly reduces the water available to downstream neighbors for drinking and household use, the downstream neighbors could challenge the farmer's use as being unreasonable.

2) Prior Appropriation

The prior appropriation doctrine, followed in many western states, dictates that water belongs initially to the state, but the right to divert and use it can be acquired by an individual, regardless of whether their land borders the water source. Rights are determined by the priority of beneficial use. The person who first uses the water for a productive or beneficial purpose has the superior right.

Example: A rancher who first diverts water from a stream to irrigate crops has priority over later users, even if the later users live adjacent to the stream. The rancher's right is secured as long as he continues to use the water beneficially.

1) 연안권(Riparian Rights)

연안권 원칙은 물이 수로를 경계로 하는 토지 소유자에게 속한다고 규정한다. 연안 토지 소유자들은 물을 합리적으로 사용할 권리를 공유하며, 다른 연안 소유자들의 물 사용을 실질적으로 방해할 수 없다. 연안권 시스템 하에서는 가정용 사용(예: 가정 내 사용)이 상업적 사용(예: 관개나 산업)보다 우선하며, 합리적인 한도 내에서 무제한으로 사용할 수 있다.

예시: 농부가 자신의 토지와 경계를 이루는 하천에서 관개를 위해 물을 전용하였는데, 이로 인해 하류의 이웃들이 음용 및 가정용으로 사용할 수 있는 물의 양이 크게 줄어든 경우, 하류의 이웃들은 농부의 사용이 불합리하다고 이의를 제기할 수 있다.

2) 선점권(Prior Appropriation)

많은 서부 주에서 따르는 선점권 원칙은 물이 처음에는 국가에 속하지만, 물의 원천과 인접한 토지 소유 여부와 관계없이 개인이 물을 전용해 사용할 권리를 획득할 수 있다고 규정한다. 권리는 유익한 사용의 우선순위에 따라 결정된다. 생산적이거나 유익한 목적으로 물을 처음 사용한 사람이 우선권을 가진다.

예시: 작물을 관개하기 위해 처음으로 하천에서 물을 전용한 목장은 이후의 사용자들보다 우선권을 가진다. 비록 이후의 사용자들이 하천과 인접한 곳에 거주하더라도 마찬가지다. 목장의 권리는 그가 계속해서 물을 유익하게 사용하는 한 보장된다.

2. 지표수(Surface Water)

Surface water includes rainwater, melted snow, and other water that lies on the surface of the land but is not part of a river or lake.

1) Common Enemy Doctrine

A landowner is permitted to take measures to repel surface water (e.g., building dikes or drainage channels) to protect their property. Actions must not cause unnecessary harm to neighbors' property.

Example: A homeowner builds a barrier to prevent flooding in their basement. However, if the barrier redirects the water to flood a neighbor's property, the homeowner could be liable.

2) Natural Flow Theory

A landowner cannot alter the natural flow of surface water in a way that would affect neighbors. States adopting this rule increasingly apply a reasonable use standard that permits some alteration of water flow as long as the benefits outweigh the harm.

Example: A developer diverts surface water to build a road. If the diverted water causes minor, non-damaging changes to a neighbor's property, the diversion might be acceptable under a reasonable use standard.

지표수는 빗물, 녹은 눈 및 토지 표면에 존재하지만 강이나 호수의 일부가 아닌 물을 말한다.

1) 공적의 원칙(Common Enemy Doctrine)

토지 소유자는 자신의 재산을 보호하기 위해 지표수를 배제하기 위한 조치를 취할 수 있다(예: 제방이나 배수로 건설). 이러한 조치는 이웃의 재산에 불필요한 해를 끼쳐서는 안 된다.

예시: 주택 소유자가 지하실의 홍수를 방지하기 위해 장벽을 건설한다. 그러나 그 장벽이 물의 흐름을 바꾸어 이웃의 재산에 홍수를 일으킨다면, 주택 소유자는 책임을 질 수 있다.

2) 자연유수 이론(Natural Flow Theory)

토지 소유자는 이웃에게 영향을 미칠 수 있는 방식으로 지표수의 자연스러운 흐름을 변경할 수 없다. 이 원칙을 채택한 주들은 점점 더 합리적 사용 기준을 적용하여, 이익이 피해를 능가하는 한 물의 흐름을 일부 변경하는 것을 허용한다.

예시: 개발업자가 도로를 건설하기 위해 지표수를 전용한다. 전용된 물의 양이 적고, 이웃의 재산에 손해를 끼치지 않는 한, 합리적 사용 기준 하에서 그 물의 전용은 허용될 수 있다.

3. 지하수(Groundwater)

1) Reasonable Use Doctrine (Majority Rule)

Landowners may use groundwater as long as the use is reasonable and does not harm neighboring properties.

2) Absolute Ownership Doctrine (Eastern States)

This doctrine followed by some eastern states allows landowners total control over water extraction and use, even if it affects neighboring properties.

3) Prior Appropriation (Western States)

Groundwater rights are treated similarly to surface water rights, with priority given to the first person to use the water beneficially.

1) 합리적 사용 원칙(Reasonable Use Doctrine)

토지 소유자는 사용이 합리적이고 이웃의 재산에 해를 끼치지 않는 한 지하수를 사용할 수 있다(다수의견).

2) 절대 소유권 원칙 (Absolute Ownership Doctrine)

일부 동부 주에서 따르는 이 원칙은 토지 소유자가 이웃의 재산에 영향을 미치더라도 물의 추출과 사용에 대한 전적인 통제권을 갖도록 허용한다.

3) 선점권 (Prior Appropriation)

일부 서부 주에서 따르는 이 원칙은 지하수 권리는 지표수 권리와 유사하게 취급되며, 물을 유익하게 처음 사용한 사람에게 우선권이 주어진다.

C 공중권(Air Rights)

Air rights refer to a landowner's right to the use and enjoyment of the airspace above their land. While this right is not absolute or exclusive, it does provide the landowner with protection against excessive interference from external sources, such as aircraft or significant noise disturbances.

Scope of Air Rights: The amount of airspace is not unlimited as it was at common law, and it is now restricted by the state and federal governments. A landowner's air rights typically extend to a reasonable height above the property necessary for the use and enjoyment of the land.

Interference with Air Rights: A landowner may have a claim if there is a significant and unreasonable interference with the use and enjoyment of their land due to intrusions in their airspace. such intrusions may constitute a trespass, a nuisance, or a governmental taking.

공중권(air rights)은 토지 소유자가 자신의 토지 위의 공역을 사용하고 향유할 수 있는 권리를 말한다. 이 권리는 절대적이거나 배타적이지 않지만, 항공기나 심각한 소음 방해와 같은 외부의 과도한 방해로부터 토지 소유권자를 보호한다.

공중권의 범위(Scope of Air Rights): 공역의 범위는 보통법에서처럼 무제한이 아니며, 현재는 주 및 연방 정부에 의해 제한된다. 토지 소유권자의 공중권은 일반적으로 토지의 사용과 향유에 필요한 합리적인 높이까지 확장된다.

공중권에 대한 방해(Interference with Air Rights): 토지 소유권자는 공역에 대한 침해로 인해 토지의 사용과 향유에 중대한 불합리한 방해가 있는 경우 클레임을 제기할 수 있다. 이러한 침해는 무단 침입(trespass), 생활방해(nuisance) 또는 정부의 수용(governmental taking)에 해당할 수 있다.

Ⅷ | 기타 사항(OTHER MATTERS)

A 생활방해(Nuisance)

1. 사적 생활방해(Private Nuisance)

A private nuisance involves any object or activity that substantially and unreasonably interferes with another individual's use or enjoyment of his land. For an interference to qualify as a nuisance, it must arise from actions that are intentional, negligent, reckless, or stem from abnormally dangerous conduct.[8]

사적 생활방해(private nuisance)는 타인의 토지의 이용 또는 향유를 실질적이고 부당하게 방해하는 모든 물건 또는 활동을 말한다. 방해가 불법적인 생활방해로 인정되려면, 그것은 고의적, 과실, 무모하거나 또는 비정상적으로 위험한 행위에서 비롯되어야 한다.

부동산의 소유권자나 임차인 등 부동산에 대한 점유권(possessory right)을 갖는 자는 생활방해를 근거로 청구를 할 수 있다. 이는 정당한 재산 사용 및 권리를 가진 사람은 누구나 생활방해로 인해 악영향을 받을 수 있으므로 방해를 해결하기 위해 법적 구제를 구할 권리가 있어야 한다는 것을 의미한다.

8) 사적 생활방해와 공공 생활방해는 불법행위법에서 주로 다루는 영역으로 자세한 내용은 The Law of Torts (미국 불법행위법, 2024.3, 강병진 저) 도서에 설명되어 있음.

2. 공공 생활방해(Public Nuisance)

A public nuisance refers to an unreasonable interference with a right common to the general public or a considerable number of people. Typical examples of public nuisance involve activities or conditions that adversely affect the community's health, safety, and convenience on a broad scale.

A private citizen can pursue a claim for public nuisance only if he suffers unique damage that is distinct from the general inconvenience or damage suffered by members of the general public.

공공 생활방해(public nuisance)는 일반 대중 또는 상당한 수의 사람들에게 공통된 권리에 대한 비합리적인 방해를 말한다. 공공 생활방해의 대표적인 예는 지역 사회의 건강, 안전 및 편의에 광범위한 영향을 미치는 활동 또는 상태를 포함한다.

일반 대중이 겪는 일반적인 불편이나 피해와는 다른 특정한 유형의 피해(unique damage)를 겪는 경우에만 개인은 공공 생활방해에 대하여 클레임을 제기할 수 있다.

B 토지용도규제(Zoning)

Zoning is a form of land use regulation exercised by state and local governments, allowing them to control and direct the development of property within their jurisdictions. Zoning laws are primarily aimed at promoting the health, safety, and general welfare of the community and segregating incompatible land uses.

Zoning laws are typically justified under the police power of the government, which is the authority to regulate in the interest of public health, safety, and welfare. However, these regulations are subject to constitutional limitations, particularly the Fifth Amendment (Takings Clause) and the Fourteenth Amendment (Due Process and Equal Protection Clauses) of the U.S. Constitution.

토지용도규제(zoning)는 주 정부와 지방 정부가 시행하는 토지 이용 규제로서, 관할 구역 내에서 부동산 개발을 통제하고 지도할 수 있게 한다. 토지용도규제법은 주로 지역 사회의 건강, 안전, 일반 복지를 증진하고, 상충되는 토지 이용을 분리하는 것을 목표로 한다.

토지용도규제법은 공중의 건강, 안전, 복지를 위해 규제할 수 있는 권한인 정부의 경찰권(police power)에 근거하여 정당화된다. 그러나 이러한 규제는 헌법적 제한을 받으며, 특히 수정헌법 제5조(수용 조항)와 수정헌법 제14조(적법절차 조항 및 평등 보호 조항)의 적용을 받는다.

1. 토지용도규제 조례(Zoning Ordinances)

Zoning ordinances are local laws that divide municipalities into districts (e.g., residential, commercial, industrial) and regulate the use, density, height, and bulk of buildings within those districts.

Example: A typical zoning ordinance might designate a neighborhood for single-family homes, prohibiting commercial businesses from operating within that district.

토지용도규제 조례(zoning ordinances)는 지방 법률로서 자치단체를 주거, 상업, 산업 구역 등으로 나누고, 해당 구역 내에서 건물의 사용, 밀도, 높이, 부피 등을 규제한다.

예시: 전형적인 토지용도규제 조례는 한 지역을 단독 주택 지구로 지정하여, 그 구역 내에서 상업적 사업체의 운영을 금지할 수 있다.

2. 토지용도규제 권한의 제한(Limitations on Zoning Authority)

Zoning regulations must be reasonable and related to a legitimate governmental interest. If zoning laws are overly restrictive or arbitrary, they may be challenged as an unconstitutional taking under the Fifth Amendment or as violating substantive due process.

토지용도규제 규정은 합리적이어야 하며 정당한 정부의 이익과 관련이 있어야 한다. 토지용도규제법이 지나치게 제한적이거나 자의적이라면, 이는 수정헌법 제5조에 따른 위헌적 수용으로 또는 실체적 적법절차를 위반한 것으로 위헌 주장이 제기될 수 있다.

3. 예외와 변동(Exemptions and Variances)

Zoning regulations are not rigid and can be adapted in specific cases through exemptions, variances, or special-use permits.

1) Exemptions

Certain properties may be exempt from zoning laws due to their unique characteristics, such as historical landmarks or pre-existing nonconforming uses.

A pre-existing use of property that no longer complies with current zoning regulations. This use may be allowed to continue under a "grandfather clause," but significant changes or expansions might not be permitted.

2) Variances

A variance is a permission granted to an owner to deviate from the strict requirements of a zoning ordinance. To obtain a variance, the owner must show that (1) the zoning law creates a unique hardship due to the physical characteristics of the property (e.g., unusual shape, topography) and (2) the variance will not be contrary to the public welfare.

3) Special Use Permits

Special use permits (also known as conditional use permits) allow a property owner to use their land in a way that the zoning ordinance otherwise would not permit. To obtain a special use permit, the property owner must show that the proposed use will not negatively impact the surrounding community. This often involves meeting certain conditions that mitigate the potential effects of the development.

These permits are typically required for land uses that may have a greater impact on the community or adjacent properties, such as churches, schools, gas stations, or other non-residential uses in residential areas.

Example: A church or religious institution may seek a special use permit to operate in a residential neighborhood. While the residential zoning might not typically allow non-residential uses, a church could be permitted if it demonstrates that it will not generate excessive traffic or disrupt the area's character.

토지용도규제 규정은 경직된 것이 아니며, 예외, 변동 또는 특별 사용 허가를 통해 특정 사례에 적용될 수 있다.

1) 예외(Exemptions)

일부 부동산은 역사적 기념물이나 기존의 비일치적 사용(nonconforming uses)과 같은 독특한 특성으로 인해 토지용도규제법에서 면제될 수 있다.

현재의 토지용도규제 규정을 더 이상 준수하지 않는 기존의 부동산 사용은 현행 규정 불소급 조항(grandfather clause)에 따라 계속 허용될 수 있지만, 상당한 변경이나 확장은 허용되지 않을 수 있다.

2) 변동(Variances)

변동은 소유자가 토지용도규제 조례의 엄격한 요구 사항에서 벗어날 수 있도록 허가된 것이다. 변동을 얻기 위해 소유자는 (1) 토지용도규제법이 부동산의 물리적 특성(예: 특이한 형태, 지형)으로 인해 특별한 어려움을 초래한다는 것과 (2) 변동이 공공 복리에 반하지 않는다는 것을 입증해야 한다.

3) 특별 사용 허가(Special Use Permits)

특별 사용 허가(special use permits) 또는 조건적 사용 허가(conditional use permits)는 토지 소유자가 토지용도규제 조례가 허용하지 않는 방식으로 토지를 사용할 수 있도록 한다. 특별 사용 허가를 받기 위해서는, 토지 소유자가 제안된 사용이 주변 공동체에 부정적인 영향을 미치지 않을 것임을 입증해야 한다. 이는 종종 개발의 잠재적 영향을 완화하는 특정 조건을 충족하는 것을 포함한다.

이러한 허가는 교회, 학교, 주유소 또는 주거 지역 내의 기타 비주거용 사용과 같이 지역 사회나 인접 부동산에 더 큰 영향을 미칠 수 있는 토지 사용에 일반적으로 필요하다.

예시: 교회나 종교 기관은 주거 지역에서 운영하기 위해 특별 사용 허가를 신청할 수 있다. 주거용 토지용도규제가 일반적으로 비주거용 사용을 허용하지 않지만, 교회가 과도한 교통을 발생시키거나 지역의 특성을 훼손하지 않을 것을 입증하면 허가될 수 있다.

C 수용(Eminent Domain)

Eminent domain is the power of the government to take private property for public use. This power is inherent in sovereign authority and is recognized in the Fifth Amendment of the United States Constitution.[9]

수용(eminent domain)은 정부가 공공의 목적을 위해 사유 재산을 취득할 수 있는 권한이다. 이 수용 권한은 주권을 가진 주 정부의 고유 권한이며, 수정헌법 제5조에서 인정되고 있다.

9) 수용 조항(Takings Clause)에 대한 사항은 헌법에서 주로 다루는 영역으로 자세한 내용은 Constitutional Law (미국 헌법, 2024.9, 강병진 저) 도서에 설명되어 있음.

MEMO

Real Property
미국 부동산법

초 판 인 쇄 2024년 10월 14일
초 판 발 행 2024년 10월 17일
저 자 강병진 미국 뉴욕주 변호사

발 행 인 이수형
발 행 처 (주)법률신문사
출 판 등 록 1980.4.22 제6-46호
주 소 서울특별시 서초구 서초대로 396, 1402호
대 표 전 화 02-3472-0602~5
팩 스 02-3472-0606
홈 페 이 지 www.lawtimes.co.kr

I S B N 979-11-5919-040-7(93360)
정 가 27,000원